CHAPTER ONE

Understanding Instructional Leadership 1

CHAPTER TWO

STEP ONE: Establish and
Implement Instructional Goals 17

CHAPTER THREE

STEP TWO: Be There for Your Staff 31

Seven Steps to Effective Instructional Leadership

Elaine K. McEwan

CORWIN PRESS, INC.
A Sage Publications Company
Thousand Oaks, California

For information:

Corwin Press, Inc.
A Sage Publications Company
2455 Teller Road
Thousand Oaks, California 91320
E-mail: order@corwin.sagepub.com

SAGE Publications Ltd.
6 Bonhill Street
London EC2A 4PU
United Kingdom

SAGE Publications India Pvt. Ltd.
M-32 Market
Greater Kailash I
New Delhi 110 048 India

Printed in the United States of America

Library of Congress Cataloging-in-Publication Data

McEwan, Elaine K., 1941-
    Seven steps to effective instructional leadership / Elaine K. McEwan.
        p. cm.
    Includes bibliographical references and index.
    ISBN 0-8039-6665-2 (cloth : alk. paper) — ISBN 0-8039-6666-0 (pbk. : alk. paper)
    1. School principals — Self rating of.   2. Educational leadership.
    3. Teacher-principal relationships. I. Title.
  LB2831.66.M383   1998
  371.2'012 — dc21   97-35718

This book is printed on acid-free paper.

98 99 00 01 02 03   10 9 8 7 6 5 4 3 2

Production Editor: S. Marlene Head
Editorial Assistant: Kristen L. Gibson
Typesetter: Joan Gazdik Gillner
Cover Designer: Marcia M. Rosenburg

Dedication

To Dr. James Heald,
the inspiration for this book

Acknowledgments

To the following instructional leaders (from the state of Illinois and National Distinguished Principals from around the country) who completed lengthy questionnaires or who agreed to be interviewed, my special thanks. Their insights have enriched my own professional life as well as the pages of this book: Harvey Alvy, Carol Auer, James A. Blockinger, Dave Burton, Nancy C. Carbone, Gary Catalani, Maryanne Friend, Nick Friend, Christine Gaylord, Linda Hanson, Robert V. Hassan, Carolyn Hood, Alan Jones, Michael L. Klopfenstein, Stella Loeb-Munson, Brent J. McArdle, Roger Moore, Phyllis O'Connell, Michael Pettibone, Richard Seyler, James D. Shifflet, James J. Simmons, Lynn Sprick, Frances Starks, Merry Gayle Wade, Sister Catherine Wingert, and Paul C. Zaander.

I also applaud the following National Distinguished Principals whose tips and ideas are included in this book: Harry Baldwin, Diane Borgman, Amelia Cartrett, Joseph Caruselle, Paul Casciano, Francine Fernandez, Richard Fitzpatrick, Nicholas Gledich, Ann Parker, Evan Harrison, Peggy Hawse, Gary McDonald, Fred Merten, Joyce Roberts, Lou Royal, Henry Scipione, Danny Shaw, Myra Spriggs, and Alan Stephenson. The accomplishments of these outstanding instructional leaders in schools and communities across the country are legendary. I count the weekend I spent in their company in October 1991 as a high point in my professional career.

I owe my great and good friend, Don Chase, field representative for the Illinois Principals Association, a debt of gratitude for the many opportunities he afforded me to share my ideas with others and grow as an instructional leader. The ink was scarcely dry on my contract when Don was at my door recruiting me to join IPA. It was one of the best decisions I ever made.

The teachers at Lincoln School in West Chicago, Illinois, taught me how to be an instructional leader. They were forthright, honest, long-suffering, and believed that all children can learn.

To my colleague and friend, Phyllis O'Connell, I am appreciative of her right-brained reading of this manuscript and her extraordinarily creative approach to instructional leadership. Her suggestions and critique were invaluable. Other colleagues who read the manuscript and offered assistance were Tom Giles, John Patterson, and Becky Rosenthal.

My superintendent, John Hennig, first believed in my abilities, gave me the freedom to grow and change, and enabled me to become an instructional leader. I have learned much from his wise counsel and his example as a leader.

To my late husband, Richard, whose encouragement to write this book did not die when he did, I am grateful.

My final tribute I reserve for my husband, Ray Adkins, whose love, warmth, patience, gentle spirit, and unerring eye for detail have seen this book from its beginning to the final form.

About the Author

Elaine K. McEwan is a private educational consultant with the McEwan-Adkins Group offering training for school districts in leadership and team building, writing workshops for children, and parenting seminars. A former teacher, librarian, principal, and assistant superintendent for instruction in a suburban Chicago school district, she is the author of nearly two dozen books including titles for parents and teachers (*Attention Deficit Disorder*, Harold Shaw), fiction for middle-grade students (*Joshua McIntire Series*, David C. Cook), and guides for educators (*Leading Your Team to Excellence: How to Make Quality Decisions*, Corwin Press). She is the education columnist for the Oro Valley Explorer (AZ) newspaper, a contributing editor to several parenting magazines on educational issues, and can be heard on a variety of syndicated radio programs helping parents solve schooling problems.

She was honored by the Illinois Principals Association as an outstanding instructional leader, by the Illinois State Board of Education with an Award of Excellence in the Those Who Excel Program, and by the National Association of Elementary School Principals as the National Distinguished Principal from Illinois for 1991.

She received her undergraduate degree in education from Wheaton College and graduate degrees in library science and educational administration from Northern Illinois University.

McEwan lives with her husband and business partner E. Raymond Adkins in Oro Valley, Arizona.

Introduction

In the fall of 1983 I was hired as the principal of an elementary school in a far western suburb of Chicago. It was my first principalship, and I was armed with five "dress for success" suits and matching bow ties, a newly acquired doctoral degree, and all of the answers. Confronted with a student body that was over one-third poor and forty percent minority, with standardized achievement test scores that hovered at the twentieth percentile, and a staff that seemed powerless in the face of such odds, I discovered that my answers were for a totally different set of questions from those I now faced.

I began to search for new answers and found them in places both expected (the research literature) and unexpected (the collective wisdom of the faculty). Research in the early eighties increasingly demonstrated the impact of the building principal's leadership. But the challenge was how to translate that research into action in my local school. I did not have years of experience upon which to draw, nor did I have unlimited staff development funds to train teachers and import new programs. In my ignorance I did not realize my limitations; I only knew what I wanted my school to become. That is always the challenge for the principal—how to create a worthy vision, and how to motivate and inspire a disparate group of students, teachers, and parents toward that vision. I discovered that the faculty could be energized and empowered by a combination of shared decision making, instructional support and encouragement, and the partnership of community businesses. Together we discovered that "the wizard was truly within us."

In the eight years I served as building principal, student achievement rose dramatically, parental involvement as measured by PTA membership and financial support tripled, and our image in the community was reversed. In just four years the percentage of students reading above grade level as measured on the Iowa Test of Basic Skills rose from 47 percent to 67 percent, and the percentage of students in the bottom quarter decreased from 30 percent to 14 percent. Mathematics scores improved similarly (53 percent to 69 percent increase in students above grade level and 27 percent to 10 percent decrease in students in the bottom quarter).

Teachers participated in planning and decision making through a building leadership team. The faculty came to view their principal as a leader rather than a manager. Decisions were no longer made unilaterally; the group participated and was held accountable. Rather than following recipes and rules that were no longer working, we hypothesized, problem solved, and tested new ideas. We focused on outcomes rather than textbooks, and expectations moved from a belief that "some can learn" to the belief that "all can learn." During my eight-year tenure, I became a student of the instructional leadership literature and dedicated myself to becoming an "instructional leader." I constantly monitored and evaluated my own behaviors, and asked my faculty to share their observations and suggestions with me, both informally and with standardized instruments. In 1989 I was privileged to be named an Instructional Leader by the Illinois Principals Association, and in 1991 I was honored to be named the National Distinguished Principal from Illinois by the National Association of Elementary School Principals. Above all else, these experiences were humbling, since they put me in touch with dozens of exemplary instructional leaders around my state and the country whose success in leading schools to excellence was awe inspiring. Many of their best practices and ideas are included in the chapters that follow.

I believe that any dedicated educator has the capability to become an exemplary instructional leader. All that one needs are the willingness to learn and the commitment to follow through in day-to-day behavior. The seven steps to effective instructional leadership discussed in the following chapters have been tested by practitioners and validated by research. Adopted, practiced, and refined in your own professional life, they are guaranteed to make a positive difference in the lives of students, teachers, and parents in your educational community. You will discover that "the wizard is truly within you."

Chapter One sets forth the differences between leadership and instructional leadership and defines the critical attributes of the latter. Chapters Two through Eight describe the seven steps in detail, offering practical suggestions about how actual principals put the steps into action in a variety of school settings—rural, urban, or suburban, and high school, middle school, or elementary. Each chapter also contains detailed behavioral indicators related to each step that will enable you to evaluate yourself and solicit feedback from the teachers with whom you work. Chapter Nine offers practical ways in which you can begin to implement the seven steps. A detailed reading list and the complete Instructional Leadership Behavioral Checklist are also included to assist you in a personal learning program.

CHAPTER ONE

Understanding Instructional Leadership

WHAT IS LEADERSHIP?

HOW DOES INSTRUCTIONAL LEADERSHIP DIFFER?

WHAT DOES RESEARCH SAY?

CAN ANY PRINCIPAL BECOME AN INSTRUCTIONAL LEADER?

WHAT ARE THE BARRIERS?

WHAT ARE THE SEVEN STEPS TO EFFECTIVE
INSTRUCTIONAL LEADERSHIP?

Thousands of school buildings dot the landscapes of America. Some have been designed by famous architects and bear historical landmark status. Others are vestiges of the cement block construction that characterized schools built for the burgeoning student population of the late fifties and early sixties. Some school buildings are located in wealthy suburban areas, while still others rise among the shattered dreams of inner city housing projects. Some serve homogeneous populations; others have hallway populations that rival the United Nations in diversity. The public earnestly desires and often stridently demands that the adults who occupy these diverse buildings on a daily basis—teachers, administrators, and other support staff—prepare young people for the future; teach children the skills they need to be successful in life; and motivate our youth to read, write, and think creatively. Many schools accomplish these

1

goals irrespective of their physical location or the demographics of the students they serve. These schools can be characterized by any number of adjectives—including *effective, excellent,* and *outstanding.* There are, however, some that can be described in less than flattering terms—such as *poor, ineffective,* or just plain *mediocre.*

Researchers have long been fascinated with the differences between effective and ineffective schools. The possibility of fixing "broken" schools or improving mediocre ones by manipulating key variables in the school environment is a tantalizing prospect for educational reformers. And while each researcher has generated a different set of descriptors that characterize effective or excellent schools, one variable always emerges as critically important: the leadership abilities of the building principal, particularly in the instructional arena. The Illinois state legislature even went so far as to mandate that building principals spend at least fifty-one percent of their time being "instructional leaders."

In this chapter, we will examine leadership in the broad sense and instructional leadership specifically, then set forth seven steps that help you to become a more effective instructional leader.

What is leadership?

Leadership is an endlessly fascinating topic. Sports fans, school board members, stockholders, and academicians all have theories about what constitutes a leader. Although many well-known definitions of leadership are included in this chapter, the classic one by Tannenbaum, Weschler, and Massarik still encompasses the most critical dimensions of leadership: "Interpersonal influence directed through the communication process toward the attainment of some goal or goals."[1] *Defining* leadership has never been a problem for researchers and theorists; discovering how to create or produce leaders has been a little more difficult. The classical theorists debated whether leadership was a function of the individual and his or her characteristics or whether the historical context served to shape the individual in response to societal needs or events.

Most contemporary researchers, however, have found it far more constructive to study what leaders actually *do* than to focus on traits such as intelligence, friendliness, or creativity. What causes one individual to lead his or her organization (business, school, sports team) to greatness while another individual, although equally intelligent, friendly, and competent, manages to achieve only mediocrity? Why are some individuals highly effective leaders in some settings while in others they are only marginally successful?

Bass lists the characteristics that differentiate leaders from followers as "a strong drive for responsibility and task completion, vigor and persistence in pursuit of goals, venturesomeness and originality in problem solving, the drive to exercise initiative in social situations, self-confidence and sense of personal identity, willingness to accept consequences of decisions and action, readiness to absorb interpersonal stress, willingness to tolerate frustration and delay, the ability to influence other persons' behavior, and the capacity to structure social interaction systems to the purpose at hand."[2] Some theorists have hypothesized that effective leaders not only possess many of these characteristics, *but* they are also able to match their leadership style to the unique needs of the situation. Rather than behaving the same way in every setting, effective leaders assess each situation and adjust their leadership behaviors to both the complexity of the task or goal as well as the composition and characteristics of the group they are leading.

Our most recent understanding of leadership has been expanded to include still another dimension—the concept of vision. Warren Bennis and Burt Nanus have enlarged the

"Nurture is far more important than nature in determining who becomes a successful leader.... Learning to be a leader is somewhat like learning to be a parent or a lover; your childhood and adolescence provide you with basic values and role models."

Warren Bennis and Burt Nanus

definition of leadership to include more than just doing things right. "Managers are people who do things right and leaders are people who do the right thing. The difference may be summarized as activities of vision and judgment—effectiveness versus activities of mastering routines—efficiency."[3] Bennis defines vision as "the capacity to create and communicate a view of the desired state of affairs that induces commitment among those working in the organization."[4] Tom Peters and Nancy Austin have pushed the definition of leadership still further. They propose that the model of manager as "cop, referee, devil's advocate, dispassionate analyst, professional decision-maker, naysayer, and pronouncer" be put to rest and that the model of leader as "cheerleader, enthusiast, nurturer of champions, hero finder, wanderer, dramatist, coach, facilitator, and builder" replace it.[5]

Leadership models have traditionally been developed and tested in the business world. Educators feel they are being encouraged to emulate Sam Walton of Wal-Mart or Bill Hewlett of Hewlett-Packard. These corporate executives, however, can measure their successes in terms of bottom lines, increased sales and productivity, and rises in stock prices. Educators, particularly principals, face a different set of challenges. Although many of the lessons of leadership in the corporate world are applicable within the walls of our schools, we need our own model of leadership, one that incorporates the unique characteristics of teaching and learning. From this need has arisen a body of literature and research on a new topic, instructional leadership.

How does instructional leadership differ?

The emphasis placed on the leadership role of the principal has changed dramatically during the past ten years. An assignment given to the typical graduate student in educational administration in the seventies or early eighties was to

"Schools operated by principals who were perceived by their teachers to be strong instructional leaders exhibited significantly greater gain scores in achievement in reading and mathematics than did schools operated by average and weak instructional leaders."

Richard Andrews

4

develop a list of jobs in the seven traditional administrative task areas (staff personnel, pupil personnel, school-community, instructional and curriculum development, finance and business management, facilities management, and intergovernmental agency relations) as they relate to the four classic management functions (planning, organizing, leading, and controlling). Today's educational administrator in training must add an additional assignment—to become an instructional leader. In a recent study of over five hundred Illinois school principals, these behaviors/tasks/skills were identified as being most critical to success in the principalship:

- Evaluating staff performance
- Setting high expectations for students and staff
- Modeling high professional standards
- Establishing and maintaining vision, mission, and goals
- Maintaining positive interpersonal relationships
- Maintaining a visible presence
- Establishing a safe and orderly environment
- Developing a school improvement plan
- Establishing an internal communications system
- Interviewing candidates for teaching positions
- Complying with mandated educational programs[6]

Thomas Sergiovanni proposed one of the first models of instructional leadership. He identified five leadership forces: (1) technical, (2) human, (3) educational, (4) symbolic, and (5) cultural.[7]

The technical aspects of instructional leadership deal with the traditional practices of management—the topics usually covered in an administrative theory course, such as planning, time management, leadership theory, and organizational development. The human component encompasses all of the interpersonal aspects of instructional leadership essential to the communicating, motivating, and facilitating roles of the principal. The educational force involves all of the instructional

"The task of leadership is to create the moral order that binds them [leaders] and the people around them."

Thomas B. Greenfield

5

aspects of the principal's role—teaching, learning, and implementing the curricula. The symbolic and cultural forces are perhaps the most elusive in terms of description and understanding. They derive from the instructional leader's ability to become the symbol of what is important and purposeful about the school (symbolic) as well as to articulate the values and beliefs of the organization over time (cultural).

The technical and human leadership skills, according to Sergiovanni, are generic. They are not unique to schools and should be present in any organization where strong leadership is evident. Effective leaders, regardless of the setting, need planning and time management skills as well as the ability to organize and coordinate. Whether the players are teachers or engineers, the effective leader needs to be skilled in providing support and encouragement, in helping to build consensus, and in fostering interpersonal communication.

Sergiovanni's educational, symbolic, and cultural leadership forces, however, are specific to the school setting. Principals who are instructional leaders must be knowledgeable about learning theory, effective instruction, and the curriculum—the power within the educational force. In addition, the instructional leader must be able to communicate and represent to students, teachers, and parents what is important and valuable in the school. He or she must become a symbolic force. Finally, the instructional leader must be skilled in the actual construction of a culture that specifically defines what a given school is all about. The educational, symbolic, and cultural dimensions are critical to leadership in the *school* setting. In the words of Sister Catherine Wingert, principal of St. Dorothy's School in Chicago, who completed a questionnaire:

> *Instructional leadership is the creation of a climate where the principal, faculty, students, parents, and school board are able to work together to accomplish the task of education.*

As the instructional leaders I interviewed went on to describe their responsibilities, they did not focus on the ability to use time wisely or manage the day-to-day operations of a building (these qualities are givens) but rather on vision, communication, risk taking, and commitment:

An instructional leader has a sense of purpose, and broad knowledge of the educational process and learning theories. She's a risk taker, has people skills, and unlimited energy.

Frances Starks, principal of
the Sauk School, Matteson, Illinois

An instructional leader has a passion for great teaching and a vision for what schools should be doing for children. He should have well thought out answers for three fundamental questions about schooling: How do children learn? How should we teach children? and How should we treat subject matter?

Alan Jones, principal of West Chicago Community
High School, a Blue Ribbon of Excellence school

What does research say?

Research has a great deal to say about the importance of instructional leadership. There are several different perspectives from which to study the subject:

- *School effectiveness* research—What kind of schoolwide practices help students learn and what role does the principal play in the creation and interaction of these practices?

- *Principal effectiveness* research—What are the most important characteristics of effective principals?

- *Instructional leadership* research—What practices of principals promote and support teaching and learning?

- *Organizational change* research—How can principals promote significant and lasting change in their schools?

- *Teacher effects* research—What instructional practices are most effective in bringing about student learning?

- *Curriculum alignment* research What are the best ways to organize and manage curricula?

- *Program coupling* research—What impact does the interaction of practices in the district, school, and classroom have on student learning?[8]

"The manager administers; the leader innovates. The manager has a short-range view; the leader has a long-range perspective. The manager asks how and when; the leader asks what and why. The manager accepts the status quo; the leader challenges it. The manager does things right, the leader does the right thing."

Warren Bennis

Any given research study or body of research taken in isolation may be uneven in terms of quality or fail to present a conclusive finding. However, when taken as a total body of work, all of these research bases clearly support the critical importance of the principal as instructional leader. The responsibility for teaching and learning in each of the schools across America on a daily basis clearly falls on the shoulders of the building principal.

But how can a mere principal be expected to digest, synthesize, evaluate, and put into practice on a daily basis all of the findings contained in the more than two hundred studies cited in the references just mentioned? "Just tell me what to do," replies the beleaguered principal beset by discipline problems, budget deficits, and broken-down boilers.

Persell and Cookson assisted practitioners by reviewing and synthesizing more than seventy-five studies. They reported that strong principals exhibit the following behaviors:

- They demonstrate a commitment to academic goals.
- They create a climate of high expectations.
- They function as instructional leaders.
- They are forceful and dynamic as leaders.
- They consult effectively with others.
- They create order and discipline.
- They marshal resources.
- They use time well.
- They evaluate their results.[9]

In 1985 Rutherford narrowed the list still further to four behaviors that differentiate effective principals from less effective ones. Effective principals

- Have "clear, informed visions of what they want their schools to become—visions that focus on students and their needs"
- "Translate these visions into goals for their schools and expectations for their teachers, students, and administrators"

- Do not stand back and wait for things to happen, but "continuously monitor progress"
- "Intervene in a supportive or corrective manner when this seems necessary"[10]

The most powerful research to date on the impact of strong instructional leadership comes from Andrews and Soder. Rather than merely describing instructional leadership behavior, they sought to show how this behavior affected the performance of students, particularly low-achieving students. They administered questionnaires to teachers in the sixty-seven elementary schools and twenty secondary schools of the Seattle, Washington school district. Eighteen different interactions that occur between principals and teachers were measured in four key areas: the principal as resource provider, the principal as instructional resource, the principal as communicator, and the principal as visible presence. Their findings showed that, as perceived by the teachers in the respective schools, the normal equivalent gain scores of students in schools led by strong instructional leaders were significantly greater in both total reading and total mathematics than those of students in schools rated as having average or weak leaders.[11] The mandate is clear: Principals must become strong instructional leaders. But how?

Can any principal become an instructional leader?

There is no magic recipe or failure-proof formula. Even though you are reading a book that promises to deliver seven steps to effective instructional leadership in the chapters ahead, there is no money-back guarantee or promise of future success. The mere reading of this or any other book will not turn you into Superleader overnight. The seven steps must be combined with training, time, hard work, painful setbacks, passionate dedication, and commitment. The instructional leaders I interviewed had many things to say about the process.

Chris Gaylord has been an elementary principal for nine

"There is nothing more difficult to take in hand, more perilous to conduct, or more uncertain in its success, than to take the lead in the introduction of a new order of things."

Machiavelli

years. Responding to the same instrument Andrews and Soder used in their study, her staff found her to be a "strong instructional leader." Gaylord says,

> [Any educator can be an instructional leader] if they want to and possess some basic talents/education. I can say this because I had no idea I'd "become" a principal! I was recruited and groomed and encouraged and supported! Both administration and staff cared enough to give me feedback and the essentials of the vision until I could carry it on and help develop it myself.

Carol Auer, an elementary principal for five years who has been recognized as a Those Who Excel educator in the state of Illinois, believes that all you need is *ganas*, a Spanish term she has learned from her Hispanic students, meaning that often indefinable will or desire.

Gary Catalani, a high school principal who has presented workshops on instructional leadership, believes that practical experience is critical:

> Instructional leadership is a development process. One can't be trained to be an instructional leader. Through course work and "on-the-job" learning experiences one can develop into an instructional leader.

Alan Jones has been a principal for eight years. His award-winning high school serves a multicultural population in a metropolitan suburban area. He is passionate about his philosophy of instructional leadership:

> To be an instructional leader, you must be a person who eats and sleeps teaching and learning. Instructional leaders must constantly think about how to organize a school and instruction so all children can learn.

Nick and Maryanne Friend are a dynamic duo. Between them they have twenty-seven years in elementary and middle school principalships. Their staffs named both of them as strong instructional leaders. This is their joint response:

> A person must believe in the capabilities of others and must be able to communicate this belief to others. An instructional leader must be able to

recognize what needs to be done and the best way to do it. That individual must be able to create a trust relationship, explain the vision/goal, and empower others. In addition, the instructional leader must be willing to plan, prioritize, and spend all the time necessary to realize the vision.

What are the barriers?

The research clearly shows that instructional leadership behaviors make a difference in a school's performance. How does the average practicing principal measure up? A survey of 250 principals conducted in 1989 reported these discouraging results. Forty percent of the principals surveyed seldom or never discussed school goals with students. Thirty-six percent seldom or never recognized teaching at formal ceremonies. Half of the group seldom or never modeled effective teaching techniques, and over one-third seldom or never helped teachers develop strategies for good teaching. Almost one-fourth of the principals surveyed said they seldom or never discussed assessment results with faculty. Even more dismaying than the responses of the principals themselves are the discrepancies reported between the principals' perceptions of themselves and teachers' perceptions. When asked if they spent time supervising teaching, nearly half of the principals responded in the affirmative. Teachers reported that only thirty percent of the principals did so. When asked if they spent time managing curriculum, nearly three-fourths of the principals answered yes. Teachers thought the percentage was less than half.[12]

There is a wide gap between research and practice, which suggests that some significant barriers are keeping principals from actually "doing" on a daily basis what is most effective in achieving results in America's schools. One cannot argue with Acheson and Smith's assertion: "We do not have data on *all* principals, or even *most*, but if the few thousands we have met or the several thousands whose teachers have responded to our surveys are representative, then we feel justified in stating that *many* principals do not treat instructional leadership as their prime concern, except in response to questionnaires."[13] What's holding us back?

Lack of skills and training. While many universities are restructuring their programs to provide more opportunities to develop leadership skills along with academic knowledge, there remains a gap between the academic and the real world. We cannot bury our heads and blame our lack of skills on anyone else, however. Those who want to become instructional leaders must seek out training and development opportunities through networking with colleagues, joining professional organizations, and completing personal programs of self-improvement.

Lack of support from superintendents, school boards, and community. The frustration and discouragement of some principals over the real or perceived lack of support from those around them is clearly a barrier to becoming an instructional leader:

> *I go almost every year to conventions for principals, and there's always a speech telling us we need to be education leaders, not managers. It's a great idea. And yet the system doesn't allow you to be an educational leader. Everyone wants the power to run schools in one way or another—the central office, the union, the board, the parents, the special interest groups. What's left for the principal to decide isn't always very much. There's so little we have to control or to change. The power, the authority, is somewhere else, though not necessarily the responsibility.*[14]

All of the instructional leaders interviewed for this book faced obstacles when they accepted their first principalships: colleagues who were skeptical or intimidated by their strong beliefs and determination, diminished budgets, schools demoralized by low achievement scores and undisciplined students, ironclad teacher contracts that stymied creativity and individual responsibility, ineffective teachers who seemed powerless to change. But these principals jumped the hurdles, destroyed the arguments, maneuvered around the obstacles, cajoled the naysayers, and achieved the unimaginable. Instructional leaders have the ability to visualize what a school should be and can become, and somehow do not permit themselves to be hamstrung by what others may perceive as obstacles.

Lack of vision, will, or courage. These are our biggest barriers to becoming instructional leaders. We are our own worst enemies. With vision, will, and courage, any principal can become an instructional leader. The message from successful instructional leaders is this: Anyone can be an instructional leader if he or she

- Has vision
- Has the knowledge base
- Is willing to take risks
- Is willing to put in long hours
- Is willing to change and grow constantly
- Thrives on change and ambiguity
- Can empower others

What are the seven steps to effective instructional leadership?

McEwan's Seven Steps to Effective Instructional Leadership are neither new nor revolutionary. They are variations on the themes that have been presented throughout Chapter One.

The following are McEwan's Seven Steps:

- Establish clear instructional goals.
- Be there for your staff.
- Create a school culture and climate conducive to learning.
- Communicate the vision and mission of your school.
- Set high expectations for your staff.
- Develop teacher leaders.
- Maintain positive attitudes toward students, staff, and parents.

What is new and revolutionary in this book is the approach

taken to help you integrate each of these steps into your own repertoire of behaviors on a daily basis. The problem with most descriptions of instructional leadership is their failure to define the attributes or characteristics in specific behavioral terms that principals can understand and use. Telling principals that they must communicate the mission of their schools to everyone in the school community is too vague. Principals need to know how this statement can be translated into action on Monday morning. Do they take out ads in the local paper or hire a skywriter? Research tells us that strong instructional leaders set clear instructional goals. But what does that look like in actual practice? We are told by the experts that we should be a visible presence. This sounds a little mysterious and otherworldly until you define the specific ways in which real principals achieve that goal. Each of the seven steps will be discussed in a subsequent separate chapter in which you will find

> "The leader is a person who is in a position to influence others to act and who has, as well, the moral, intellectual, and social skills required to take advantage of that position."
>
> Phillip C. Schlechty

1.	Advice from our own panel of instructional leaders on how they have implemented the step in their professional experiences
2.	Supporting data from the best research studies on what works in each step
3.	Practical suggestions for ideas to implement immediately
4.	An instructional leadership behavioral checklist that will enable you to personally assess where you fall on each behavioral continuum in anticipation of setting personal goals

The Instructional Leadership Behavioral Checklist is made up of thirty different indicators, several for each of the seven steps. You can use the checklist in a variety of ways: (1) to self-assess your present level of instructional leadership,

2) to gain information from all or selected members of your faculty with regard to their perceptions of your instructional leadership, 3) to help you set goals for improving your instructional leadership, and 4) to help you evaluate progress toward meeting the goal of becoming a true instructional leader. You can use all or parts of the checklist, depending upon your own personal progress toward becoming an effective instructional leader.

The checklist does not prescribe methodologies or improvement models. Your district may be "doing" Madeline Hunter, effective schools, mastery learning, outcomes-based education, cooperative learning, total quality management, heterogeneous grouping, site-based management, multiage grouping, or essential schools. As Terrence Deal points out, "Each approach has a cadre of gurus, scholars, advocates, and disciples who righteously defend one view against criticism from other camps. The end result is a cacophony of voices: a dialogue of the deaf among academics, usually a source of confusion among those struggling with how to improve schools."[15] Becoming an instructional leader is a goal that can be accomplished in the context of any other instructional or organizational model. This is not another layer of prescriptions. Remember that implementing the seven steps to effective instructional leadership is not something you will "do" to your school or teachers, but something you will "do" to yourself. You as a person are going to change the way you go about doing business. You will focus less on changing others and more on letting others respond to the changes you make in your own behavior. You need no one's permission to implement the seven steps. They do not cost anything or require expensive consultants. You need not even tell anyone that you are doing something new. But do not be surprised when parents, students, and teachers begin to notice. The changes you make in your own behavior will produce dramatic results in the effectiveness of your teachers, the learning of your students, and the personal satisfaction you will feel from having made a difference.

Notes

1. R. Tannenbaum, I. R. Weschler, and F. Massarik, *Leadership and Organization* (New York: McGraw-Hill, 1961), 24.

2. B. Bass, *Stogdill's Handbook of Leadership: A Survey of Theory and Research* (New York: Free Press, 1981), 81.

3. Warren Bennis and Burt Nanus, *Leaders: The Strategies for Taking Charge* (New York: Harper & Row, 1985), 21.

4. Warren Bennis, "Transformation Power and Leadership," in *Leadership and Organizational Culture*, Thomas J. Sergiovanni and John E. Corbally, eds. (Urbana-Champaign: University of Illinois Press, 1984), 66.

5. Tom Peters and Nancy Austin, *A Passion for Excellence: The Leadership Difference* (New York: Random House, 1985), 265.

6. From a study conducted by Illinois Mathematics and Science Academy (Aurora, Illinois), Mathematics Science Alliance, Motorola Corporation, and the Illinois Principals' Association, 1992.

7. Thomas J. Sergiovanni, "Leadership and Excellence in Schooling," *Educational Leadership* (February 1984): 4-13; *The Principalship: A Reflective Practice Perspective* (Boston: Allyn and Bacon, Inc., 1985).

8. Northwest Educational Cooperative, *Principals Who Produce Results: How They Think; What They Do* (Arlington Heights, Illinois: Northwest Educational Cooperative, 1985). Also Northwest Regional Educational Laboratory, *Effective Schooling Practices: A Research Synthesis* (Portland, Oregon: Northwest Regional Educational Laboratory, 1984).

9. Caroline Persell and Peter Cookson, "The Effective Principal in Action," in *The Effective Principal: A Research Summary* (Reston, Virginia: National Association of Secondary School Principals, 1982), 22.

10. William Rutherford, "School Principals as Effective Leaders," *Phi Delta Kappan* (1985): 32.

11. Richard Andrews and Roger Soder, "Principal Leadership and Student Achievement," *Educational Leadership* (March 1987): 9-11. Richard Andrews and Wilma F. Smith, *Instructional Leadership: How Principals Make a Difference* (Alexandria, Virginia: Association for Supervision and Curriculum Development, 1989).

12. Russell Ames, "Feedback Needed to Create Leadership Teams," *Leadership and Learning Newsletter* (Urbana-Champaign: University of Illinois, National Center for School Leadership, Fall 1989).

13. Keith Acheson and Stuart C. Smith, *It Is Time for Principals to Share the Responsibility for Instructional Leadership With Others* (Eugene, Oregon: Oregon School Study Council, February 1986), 19.

14. Ernest Boyer, *High School: A Report on Secondary Education in America* (New York: Harper & Row, 1983), 219.

15. Terrence Deal, "Educational Change: Revival Tent, Tinkertoys, Jungle, or Carnival," in *Rethinking School Improvement: Research, Craft, and Concept,* Anne Lieberman, ed. (New York: Teachers College Press, 1986), 115.

CHAPTER TWO

STEP ONE
Establish and Implement Instructional Goals

HOW CAN YOU ESTABLISH INSTRUCTIONAL GOALS?
HOW CAN YOU INCORPORATE OTHER CURRICULA?
HOW CAN YOU ENSURE A CONSISTENT PROGRAM?
HOW WILL YOU KNOW WHEN YOUR GOALS HAVE BEEN REACHED?
HOW CAN YOU USE THE INSTRUCTIONAL LEADERSHIP BEHAVIORAL CHECKLIST?

If we agree that the primary purpose of schooling is learning, then deciding what should be taught, how much of it should be taught, and how it should be organized for teaching are paramount goals for the effective instructional leader. Unfortunately, we often seem to spend more time in schools telling teachers how they should teach, when our concern should be what we want our students to know and be able to do when they graduate from our schools.

Decisions about what to teach were easy when textbooks were the curriculum. Principals could place one teacher's edition and thirty books for each course or subject in the hands of the teacher and depart, confident that the material was "being covered." However, establishing instructional goals for the twenty-first century is a far more daunting assignment.

Alan Jones, one of most intense instructional leaders I've

met, is a high school principal who is constantly thinking about teaching and learning. His keen intellect probes for relationships and connections. He has cleverly conveyed the challenges we face in framing both "old and new paradigm" responses to the question "How should we treat subject matter?"

Old Paradigm Responses	New Paradigm Responses
Kids need to know these facts for kindergarten (high school, college, life).	Our teachers focus on meaning from the very beginning.
I have to cover the textbook.	Schools should pick the most important concepts and skills to emphasize so they can concentrate on quality and not quantity.
Kids need to learn skills before they can learn concepts.	We try to balance routine skill learning with appropriate novel and complex tasks from the earliest stages of learning.

How can you establish instructional goals?

The instructional leader is ultimately responsible for guiding the development and implementation of a set of clear instructional goals for his or her school—broad general outcomes that define what students should know and be able to do when they exit the school. In addition to these broad goals, you will also need specific outcomes for every curricular area and grade level. These specific outcomes will constitute the road map for learning for you and your staff. They will guide the selection of materials and programs, dictate the types of instructional strategies and approaches used, and suggest the kinds of assessments needed to determine success.

You won't have to do the job alone, however. In fact, engaging your teachers, parents, community members, and even students in the process is essential and can have an energizing effect on the entire learning process. My staff and I found that defining key outcomes for students and publishing them for everyone to see and use kept us all accountable. Focusing the attention of your teachers on what students *must* be able to know and do, rather than on specific models of instruction that teachers *must* follow, will empower your teachers to choose the most effective instructional strategies and programs from among many. Your teachers won't have to be slaves to cooperative learning or Madeline Hunter's seven-step process for organizing lessons, although both are important methodologies for teachers to have in their instructional repertoires. Teachers can begin to use their own professional judgments and select the method that works best for any given situation.

Perhaps your mind has already shifted into neutral, confident that your district or state has taken care of telling your teachers what to teach. If you work in an area where learning outcomes or core curricula have been established, please don't make the mistake of thinking that handing a three-ring binder to your teachers will get the job done.

You must engage in a variety of processes to help teachers identify which of the many state and district outcomes are *most* critical for the students of your particular school. A needs assessment that combines the ideas of parents, teachers, and students can assist you in this important task. Teachers must have an opportunity to find out how the outcomes of their grade levels relate to the grade levels above and below them. Help teachers to build continuity across grade levels and courses through discussing and planning together. Work with the district and/or state outcomes until they become your school outcomes. Staff, students, and community alike must know the scope of the curricula and which aspects are critical for success in your school. Publish an abbreviated version of your outcomes in a booklet for parents, or print signs and laminate them for teachers' classrooms. Only if your staff takes personal ownership of the outcomes will they feel the accountability to translate those outcomes into student learning.

Instructional leaders such as Michael Klopfenstein who have engaged in this process attest to its success:

> *We have developed our own curricula in all areas together. We have stated what we feel is important for our young people to learn and have developed ways of assessing their progress. We did this through a process involving the business community, parents, faculty, staff, and students.*

Involving staff in developing outcomes is a time-consuming process. And once begun, it never ends. But as one instructional leader summarized, "Through this process we no longer look at each other for direction, but toward our common goals."

How can you incorporate other curricula?

Meeting the needs of the specific students who attend your school is your first and most important obligation. But you also have the responsibility to meet district and state guidelines. The motivation to focus on state goals is even more pressing if a statewide assessment is used to measure student progress. One technique that has worked well for some instructional leaders is to develop a document that places the curricular expectations into a hierarchy. The state and/or system curricula are placed at the top. These may be similar to the following State Goals for Learning in Mathematics from the State of Illinois:

- Goal 6: As a result of their schooling, students will be able to understand and apply geometric concepts and relations in a variety of forms.

- Goal 7: As a result of their schooling, students will be able to understand and use methods of data collection and analysis, including tables, charts and comparison.

Districts can develop their own general learning outcomes for each grade level, such as these for fifth grade:

- General Learning Outcome 7.1: Systematically collect, organize and analyze data from tables, charts and graphs.

- General Learning Outcome 7.2: Make inferences and evaluate arguments based on data analysis.

The general learning outcomes can then be followed by more specific learning outcomes, which can be developed at the school level:

- 7.1.1: Construct, read and analyze data included on student constructed graphs as well as those from outside sources.

- 7.2.1: Write and orally make convincing arguments based on data analysis.

What is most critical, however, is that each school develop its own specific responses to the outcomes that flow from the *needs* of its specific student body. If used properly, a well-developed state or district outcome statement/curriculum can be a powerful impetus for bringing about instructional/curricular change in a school. Rather than bemoaning the limitations of such a document, effective instructional leaders use it as a tool to find ways to improve instruction and learning.

How can you ensure a consistent program?

Lawrence Lezotte, author and researcher in the area of effective schools, has put it this way: "What gets measured gets done."[1] To the extent that you as an instructional leader are committed to the instructional goals of your school and are paying attention to their achievement, those goals will be accomplished.

Instructional leadership takes courage. Ensuring that school and classroom activities are consistent with school instructional

"When teachers prepare their own curriculum outlines, crucial issues come to the surface and promote examination of what teachers believe about themselves, about children, and about teaching."

Roland Barth

goals and objectives means that you as a principal will expect every teacher to teach and every student to learn. And when that doesn't happen, you'll be there to ask why as well as provide support and encouragement for finding possible answers. Put teams of teachers together to solve grade-level or course problems. The pressures that marginal teachers will feel to measure up will encourage them to seek out resources and alternative instructional strategies. Let "teacher power" assist you in improving the marginal teacher. Set group goals and measure group progress. No one will want to be left behind. What you and your faculty choose to pay attention to, determine is important, and measure and monitor will be accomplished more effectively than it ever was in the past.

How will you know when your goals have been reached?

If your goal is student learning, what benchmarks will you use to determine success? The research is clear about the importance of monitoring learning progress:[2]

- Use test results, grade reports, attendance records, and other information to spot potential problems. Become skilled at picking up bits and pieces of information as you talk with teachers, attendance clerks, counselors, or deans. Move in on potential instructional or learning problems swiftly. There's no time for a "wait and see" attitude when a child's academic success is at stake.

- No matter who teaches a course or what methodologies are used, the outcomes should be consistent. Facilitate the development of common final examinations in core courses taught by many different teachers. These exams will provide teachers with a focus, result in better tests, and enable you, the instructional leader, to monitor the consistency in your curriculum.

- Share summaries of student performance with all of the staff who can then assist in developing action alternatives. All of the teachers in your school are responsible for all of the students. The kindergarten teachers should be interested in the achievement of sixth graders and vice versa. Teachers of seniors should feel as responsible for freshman course outlines as they do about their own. Work to eliminate the "closed door" syndrome where teachers feel no responsibility for what is happening in other classrooms of the building. Target low- or underachieving students in your school for an all-out team effort to improve achievement. Make the target students the responsibility of all faculty. Form a problem-solving child-study team to come up with innovative instructional strategies to help these students. Find ways to offer extra help and increased opportunities for success.

- Collect trend data so that you can evaluate your progress toward goals over several years. One year of data rarely is enough to draw conclusions. Learn to use a computer and become proficient at developing graphs and charts.

- Collect data from other sources in addition to student achievement, such as staff development participation, teacher appraisals, staff attendance, parental involvement in PTA, school volunteers, and attendance at parent-school activities.

- Survey the faculty, community, and student body relative to their perceptions about the school's effectiveness.

- Report scores in a useful format. Lorin Anderson offers an excellent idea for presenting lots of data in an understandable way. He suggests that percents always paint a clear picture:

For teacher-made tests, the percent of students achieving grades of A or B would be presented. For curriculum-embedded tests, the percent of students mastering each objective would be presented. For state proficiency/competency tests, the percent of students who meet or exceed the overall standard would be presented. Finally, for nationally normed, commercially produced tests, the percent of students who fall in the highest and lowest national quartiles would be presented.[3]

- If your community or state doesn't issue a report card on student achievement, publish your own school report card so that parents are aware of your emphasis on accountability. Communicate student progress to parents through printed reports, parent conferences, narratives, and portfolios that give a holistic picture of student strengths and weaknesses.

- Match your assessments to learning outcomes and do your best to coordinate your school-, district-, and state-level tests to minimize the amount of time spent in testing.

- Disaggregate different types of data to determine if all students have an equal chance of achieving academic success in your school. Disaggregation is the process of separating out different types of information for different groups of students (e.g., Do a higher percentage of boys score in the upper quartiles in math and science than girls? or Are specific ethnic groups overrepresented in the lower quartiles on standardized achievement tests?) Types of data that can be disaggregated include: norm-referenced test scores, criterion-referenced test scores, state-level test scores, grade distributions, attendance/tardiness patterns; graduation rates; expulsions; students accepted in postsecondary education programs; graduates placed in jobs; students participating in extracurricular activities; students receiving academic awards and scholarships; discipline referrals, suspensions, advanced-placement enrollments; specific courses (e.g., algebra); and honor roll. Student groups to pull out for comparison might include: higher/lower socioeconomic status, minority/nonminority, gender, student mobility, special programs (Chapter One; Special Education), or placement levels in classes.

- Update student records in a timely fashion so that all individuals who work with a student will have relevant information at their fingertips.

- Use less traditional methods of gathering data, such as flow charts, histograms, scattergrams, and force field analyses, as described by John Jay Bonstingl.[4]

The effective instructional leaders we interviewed spend a

lot of time evaluating their effectiveness in reaching academic goals and they have clear ideas of what constitutes success.

Linda Hanson has led her high school toward performance-based assessments. She explains:

> *We are starting some pretty sophisticated outcomes-based assessments in some areas. If students can accomplish the outcomes, we've achieved our goals.*

Dave Burton, a middle school principal, doesn't rely on just one measure. He's constantly assessing, especially during his frequent forays into the hallways, cafeteria, and team planning periods. He says:

> *I look at the analysis of standardized test scores, review student grades quarterly, make frequent classroom observations, and talk with teachers and students almost daily.*

Instructional leadership is not like running a race. There is never a clear finish with a declared winner. Schools are organizations in constant flux. The staff changes, as do the students and curricula. As one instructional leader told me, we must keep monitoring and adjusting to reflect this process:

> *I'm not sure that some goals are ever reached—you usually are shooting at a moving target. It's important to see progress toward your goals. It may not be a goal that has closure, but if you're seeing progress you're being successful.*

But everyone agrees that the bottom line is student performance. James Shifflet put it this way: "When our students are successful, we are successful."

> "Historically, schools and school systems would be reaccredited and even receive public acclaim if they had the appropriate mix of inputs (books in the library) and curricular offerings (advanced math courses). Unfortunately, these input assessments never addressed the question of how much students were actually learning at the school."
>
> Lawrence W. Lezotte

How can you use the Instructional Leadership Behavioral Checklist to assess your progress toward Step One: Establish and implement instructional goals?

There are four indicators that describe Step One in more detail:

1.	Involves teachers in developing and implementing school instructional goals and objectives
2.	Incorporates the designated state and/or system curricula in the development of instructional programs
3.	Ensures that school and classroom activities are consistent with school instructional goals and objectives
4.	Evaluates progress toward instructional goals and objectives

Each indicator is followed by three sections:

1.	A **comment** that defines the specifications of the indicator
2.	A **scale of descriptors** that gives a continuum of behaviors (1-5) from least effective to most effective
3.	**Key points in the descriptors** that give detailed explanations of each of the five items in the scale

For each indicator, select the number from 1 to 5 that most accurately describes your own behavior on a day-to-day basis.

"Much of what schools are trying to teach—the ability to write, to speak, to create, to demonstrate tolerance, to make responsible decisions—simply cannot be measured by a multiple-choice test. School leaders must work with teachers to identify and develop indicators of student achievement with respect to such goals."

Richard P. DuFour and Robert Eaker

INSTRUCTIONAL LEADERSHIP
BEHAVIORAL CHECKLIST

STEP ONE: Establish and implement
instructional goals.

Indicator 1.1 Involves teachers in developing and implementing school instructional goals and objectives

---

Comment:

The main focus of Indicator 1.1 is the involvement of teachers with the principal in the development and implementation of instructional goals and objectives.

SCALE OF DESCRIPTORS:

1. Curriculum is textbook driven, and neither principal nor teachers have involvement in the development of instructional goals.

2. Principal makes all decisions regarding instructional goals and objectives with no input from faculty.

3. Faculty input is solicited and/or received from time to time, but no organized system for developing instructional goals is in place, and unilateral decisions regarding curricula are frequently made.

4. Principal and faculty have worked together in a systematic fashion to establish achievement objectives (learner outcomes), but implementation of objectives is an individual classroom activity.

5. Principal and faculty have jointly established specific achievement objectives, and faculty members share responsibility for the buildingwide implementation of these objectives.

KEY POINTS IN DESCRIPTORS:

1. No involvement of either teachers or principal

2. No involvement of teachers

3. Minimal involvement of teachers

4. Joint involvement of teachers and principal in development

5. Joint involvement of teachers and principal in development and implementation

Indicator 1.2 Incorporates the designated state and/or system curricula in the development of instructional programs

27

Comment:

The main focus of Indicator 1.2 is the support the principal gives to mandated state and local programs while designing an instructional program that meets the needs of the individual school and/or classroom.

SCALE OF DESCRIPTORS:

1. Principal does not support the incorporation of state and/or system curricula into the instructional program.

2. Principal feels that state and/or system curricula should be included in the instructional program but permits teachers to exercise personal judgments regarding their ultimate inclusion.

3. Principal feels that state and/or system curricula should be included and communicates these expectations to teachers.

4. Principal feels that state and/or system curricula should be included, communicates these expectations to teachers, and works with them in the development of instructional programs that do this effectively.

5. Principal feels that state and/or system curricula should be included, communicates these expectations to teachers, works with them in the development of instructional programs that do this effectively, and monitors classroom activities to ensure such inclusion.

KEY POINTS IN DESCRIPTORS:

1. No incorporation of state or system curricula into program

2. Belief in importance but permissive in supervision

3. Belief in importance with expectations communicated

4. Belief in importance, expectations communicated, assistance provided

5. Belief in importance, expectations communicated, assistance provided, and implementation monitored

Indicator 1.3 Ensures that school and classroom activities are consistent with school instructional goals and objectives

Comment:

The main focus of Indicator 1.3 is the match between instructional goals and what is happening in individual classrooms and the school as a whole, and what the principal is doing to ensure that consistency exists throughout the building. The existence of clear instructional goals is a given in this indicator.

SCALE OF DESCRIPTORS:

1. Although school instructional goals and objectives do exist, many activities appear to act as deterrents and/or impediments to the achievement of goals and objectives.

2. Although school instructional goals and objectives do exist, activities in the school as a whole (majority of classrooms) do not appear to support these objectives.

3. Although activities in the school as a whole appear to support the stated instructional goals and objectives, there are many individual classrooms in which activities do not support school goals.

4. Activities in most classrooms and the school as a whole appear to support the stated instructional goals and objectives.

5. Activities in all classrooms and the school as a whole appear to support the stated instructional goals and objectives.

KEY POINTS IN DESCRIPTORS:

1. Unwilling to address a lack of consistency in *many* classrooms (more than half) or in the *school as a whole*

2. Expresses a verbal willingness to address lack of consistency but fails to follow through with actions to ensure consistency

3. Willing to address a lack of consistency between goals and activities but marginally effective in doing so

4. Willing to ensure consistency between goals and activities and usually very effective in doing so

5. Highly effective in ensuring that activities match objectives

Indicator 1.4 Evaluates progress toward instructional goals and objectives

Comment:

The main focus of Indicator 1.4 is the use of a combination of evaluation methods, and if needed, subsequent adjustments in the program to ensure that goals and objectives are being met.

SCALE OF DESCRIPTORS:

1. No schoolwide program of testing exists.

2. Although a schoolwide standardized testing program exists, this information is used in a general systemwide way and the principal does not use the information to evaluate the school program.

3. Standardized test information is the sole indicator used by the principal for program evaluation. Review of the information is not systematic or specific, and teachers rarely review the results beyond the initial report.

4. The results of multiple-assessment methods such as mastery skills checklists, criterion-referenced tests, standardized tests, and performance or portfolio assessments are systematically used and reviewed by the principal along with teachers.

5. Results of multiple-assessment methods are systematically used to evaluate program objectives. Teachers and principals analyze the results and together make program modifications.

KEY POINTS IN DESCRIPTORS:

1. No standardized testing program

2. Standardized testing program with little utilization of results by either principal or teachers

3. Standardized testing program with some utilization of results by principal and little utilization of results by teachers

4. Well-rounded evaluation program with some utilization of results by both principal and teachers

5. Well-rounded evaluation program with effective utilization of results by both principal and teachers to modify and improve program

Notes

1. Presentation to the Administrative Staff of West Chicago Elementary District #33, October 1985.

2. Northwest Regional Educational Laboratory, *Effective Schooling Practices: A Research Synthesis* (Portland, Oregon: Northwest Regional Educational Laboratory, 1984).

3. Lorin Anderson, "Frequent Monitoring of Student Progress," paper presented at South Carolina Conference on Public Schools, (Charleston, South Carolina, 1985).

4. John Jay Bonstingl, *Schools of Quality: An Introduction to Total Quality Management in Education* (Alexandria, Virginia: Association for Supervision and Curriculum Development, 1992), 51-68.

CHAPTER THREE

Step Two
Be There for
Your Staff

HOW CAN YOU WORK WITH TEACHERS?

HOW CAN YOU SHARE RESEARCH?

HOW CAN YOU APPLY ASSESSMENT PROCEDURES?

IS IT POSSIBLE TO KNOW WHAT IS GOING ON IN EVERY CLASSROOM?

HOW CAN YOU USE THE INSTRUCTIONAL LEADERSHIP BEHAVIORAL CHECKLIST?

How can you work with teachers?

Effective instructional leaders function as unique amalgams of ombudsmen, reference librarians, and genies-in-a-bottle who are constantly helping faculty to find the solutions they need to frustrating and difficult instructional problems. Problems are solved in brainstorming sessions, structured meetings, and brief hallway encounters. Instructional leaders rarely say no to new ideas as they encourage teachers to try alternative techniques without fear of failure. As active listeners, instructional leaders help teachers reflect on their own teaching and empower them to reach out for personal solutions. Their office doors are generally open, and when instructional leaders talk with teachers, they do things like clear their tables of other work, take notes, paraphrase, and give feedback. They are willing to share ownership of any teacher's problem and do not point fingers, assign blame, or become judgmental.

31

Instructional leaders are also resource providers adept at finding and allocating money, planning and developing programs, and motivating both parents and community to become involved with their schools. Constantly on the lookout for opportunities, such leaders are masters at "working the crowd." They are prolific grant writers, and when they see a need, they find a way; they do not know the meaning of the word *no*. They build school-business partnerships, seek out community support, and champion the causes of their school to anyone who will listen. Instructional leaders also know the importance of fostering harmonious and productive relationships with superintendents, curriculum directors, and other staff resource people; all of these individuals can help the instructional leader offer more resources to his or her staff.

Effective instructional leaders do all of these things and more by utilizing the four Cs—Collaboration, Collegiality, Cooperation, and Creative Problem Solving. Their calendars are filled with meetings that focus on the four Cs:

- A meeting with the child-study team to brainstorm solutions to a learning problem (result: a plan to try a different instructional methodology in the area of reading)
- A meeting with the building leadership team to facilitate the evolution of staff development goals (result: the development of goals in peer coaching and mentoring for the faculty)
- A meeting between parents of a gifted student, the library learning center teacher, the classroom teacher, and the student (result: an independent research project to support classwork that will involve field trips with the parents)
- A meeting with the math department about the new state assessment (result: department chair will attend workshop and bring back materials and present workshop to rest of staff)
- A meeting with the fifth grade team to discuss the implementation of the new math program (result:

acquisition of more materials to help with concepts in fractions and bringing in a math consultant to do a demonstration lesson for each teacher)

Rarely does the instructional leader enter a meeting room with a preconceived idea about how a problem should be solved; yet in each case, through collaboration, cooperation, collegiality, and creative problem solving, the participants emerge feeling empowered and energized.

How can you share research?

Instructional leaders take personal responsibility for making sure that research and successful practices are talked about frequently and demonstrated ably in their schools. They make it happen. But they don't do it all by themselves. Maryanne Friend encourages teachers to share their talents:

> *To take advantage of this often neglected resource, I began to have a sharing time at each staff meeting. Last year the sharing was voluntary. Several of the "sharing" teachers put together a presentation for a district inservice. This year, sharing is required.*

Paul Zaander asks teachers who attend workshops to make presentations when they return. He also arranges with a local university to hold classes in his building, thereby ensuring a high degree of participation from his teachers. Andy Bertram encourages his teachers to pursue advanced degrees and even sorts the mail himself so he can make sure that the appropriate flyers and advertisements for staff development opportunities get into the right mailboxes.

Effective instructional leaders are eager learners. They read a variety of publications, attend workshops and national conferences, present staff development programs to their staffs, and are constantly on the lookout for potential resources for their buildings. They keep a file of speakers, articles, and ideas to pull out when the right moment presents itself in a conversation with a teacher.

Many instructional leaders conduct action research in their

own buildings with local colleges or foundations. Carol Auer and her faculty have teamed up with the Ball Foundation of Glen Ellyn, Illinois, to find out if student achievement will be affected by increased parent-teacher contacts that take place in alternative settings such as homes, restaurants, or the workplace.

Here are a variety of other ways in which effective instructional leaders introduce their teachers to learning opportunities:

- Provide copies of pertinent articles in teachers' mailboxes. Don't overdo this practice or your paper budget will explode. But do find ways to work into conversations and presentations the findings of the research you think may have bearing on programs in your school. Teachers will soon discover "what's hot and what's not" and will begin reading on their own. A word of caution: Make it clear to staff that you are simply expanding their views and encouraging them to think. When an idea or strategy has the potential for schoolwide implementation, reassure teachers that plenty of brainstorming, discussion, problem solving, and decision making will take place before implementation.

- Ask a local university to place student teachers in your building. Working with an enthusiastic young educator who has been recently trained can often be a motivator for a veteran staff member.

- Act as a "seed planter" in your school. When you see an example of outstanding teaching or a particularly creative lesson, ask the teacher's permission to share the idea with someone else. Teachers who might be reticent to "brag" about their own work are usually delighted when the principal does it for them.

- Encourage teachers to do term papers and other class projects for their advanced-degree work on topics of interest/concern to the faculty. Ask them to share. One of my teachers who was working on her doctorate in curriculum and instruction researched the issue of homework and its effectiveness when we were preparing our school homework policy. Many universities offer field-based degree programs. Assist your teachers in choosing their areas of study to maximize the impact on your school.

"Students benefit academically when their teachers share ideas, cooperate in activities, and assist one another's intellectual growth."

What Works

- Plan a yearly overnight, a weekend retreat, or just a casual gathering at someone's home. These times away are perfect to talk about new ideas or develop goals for the coming year. Instructional leaders find it helpful to get people into a relaxed setting removed from the pressures and time crunches that characterize so many faculty gatherings.

- Purchase videotapes that emphasize topics/instructional strategies/curricula that you are highlighting. Organize a systematic circulation program so that everyone has a chance to view them. Schedule a roundtable discussion at faculty meetings.

- Encourage staff members to develop expertise in certain areas so they can function as specialists on your staff. Include topics in department meetings that encourage department chairpersons to share information and experiences.

- Encourage teachers who are willing to pilot programs or instructional strategies in their classrooms so they can share with others who may need more help and encouragement.

- Take advantage of every opportunity to share your values about teaching and learning—through what you write in evaluation instruments, what you say in postobservation conferences, how you interact in brief hallway encounters, and what you choose to focus on in formal staff development presentations.

How can you apply assessment procedures?

This aspect of instructional leadership can best be described as the day-to-day, week-to-week assessment of how well the instructional program is meeting the needs of individual students. You are essentially dipsticking in every classroom, and sometimes even into the learning of individual students in each classroom. In "managing by walking around," you are putting your finger on the collective pulse of the school and finding out if the heart is still beating. Is everybody on track? Is everybody keeping the faith?

This key question must be asked of every teacher on a regular basis: "How are things going in your classroom?" This question is asked *not* to evaluate the teacher's performance but to ascertain what else you as the instructional leader could be doing to help that teacher. Focus not on the teacher but on the goals that have been established by that grade level/department/team. You are asking the questions not to judge but to make sure that you are aware at any given time of the "hot spots" in your building. Which classrooms need your presence? Which classrooms need the behavior management specialist for consultation? Who needs the services of an instructional aide? Who needs additional resources to accomplish their goals? Accompanying questions might also include:

- Do you have all the materials you need to get the job done?
- Are all of the children in your class learning
- Do you have any serious behavior problems?
- Is there anything about this year that surprises you?
- What's your best success story so far?
- What has you most frustrated?
- How's the new math program (or any other new program) working? Any concerns?
- Is there anything I can do to help?

Some teachers, especially those who are confident and resourceful, will share with you regularly about what is going on in their classrooms. They will delight in reporting their successes and enlisting your help with problems. But others, particularly if the school culture has not always supported openness and sharing, will be reticent to share problems with the principal. They may feel they are complaining or that their problems will be tallied up for a subsequent write-up on an evaluation. These attitudes will change as your staff comes to know, respect, and trust you as an instructional leader.

Is it possible to know
what is going on in every classroom?

"The more knowledgeable you are about what is happening in the classrooms, the more effective you can be." Instructional leaders such as Paul Zaander push themselves to be out in classrooms. They call it "being there" for the teachers. Often their paperwork suffers, but instructional leaders frequently stay in the office after everyone has left the building to tackle the "paper piles" that inevitably develop during each day. Frequent drop-ins of ten to fifteen minutes per classroom enable principals to cover at least five to seven classrooms per day. Some carry a clipboard to keep records of the drop-ins or notes of things to do when they return to the office. The knowledge they acquire while "wandering" enables them to support teachers and to get to know students in different ways. Principals of large elementary schools, middle schools, or high schools have more classrooms to cover, but with the assistance of support personnel, the job can be done. "There is no substitute for getting into classrooms and seeing what is going on," says high school principal Alan Jones. "One postconference is worth a thousand memos on effective instruction."

Merry Gayle Wade refuses to let the "administrivia" of a building principalship get her down. "Fifty percent of my time is spent visiting classrooms and an additional twenty-five percent working with teachers to improve their teacher effectiveness skills." Carol Auer has classroom visitation as her number one priority as well. "There is always some other thing that needs attending to—in fact, one hundred other things, but if observing is important to you, you find the time to spend in the classroom."

Instructional leaders do more than just walk through the classrooms. They read stories, act as aides, and teach units of instruction as well. But no matter what they are doing, it is their visible presence that matters. Nancy Carbone feels "it

> "If teachers talked more with each other about both education and students, the chances for productive exchange about the effects of their efforts on students would increase."
>
> Arthur G. Powell, Eleanor Farrar, and David K. Cohen

sends a signal to the entire staff that good instruction and the carrying out of curriculum goals are important."

Instructional leaders spend more time in the classrooms of teachers they perceive as weak or needing help. Harvey Alvy suggests that "when you hire good folks, you need to have faith in them, but with marginal staff, you need to know everything that's going on." Although they may not visit every classroom every day, effective instructional leaders have a strong sense of what is happening in each classroom. Student and parent opinions help to shape these perceptions and so do frequent conversations with staff about their beliefs and values with regard to teaching and learning. But nothing beats firsthand knowledge. "The only way to get to the heart of the matter is to be there. The classroom is the heart and soul of the school and to keep a finger on the pulse, you must be in the classroom," says high school principal Gary Catalani.

How can you use the Instructional Leadership Behavioral Checklist to assess your progress toward Step Two: Be there for your staff?

There are three indicators that describe Step Two in more detail:

1.	Works with teachers to improve the instructional program in their classrooms consistent with student needs
2.	Bases instructional program development on sound research and practice
3.	Applies appropriate formative procedures in evaluating the instructional programs

Each indicator is followed by three sections:

1.	A **comment** that defines the specifications of the indicator
2.	A **scale of descriptors** that gives a continuum of behaviors (1-5) from least effective to most effective
3.	**Key points in the descriptors** that give detailed explanations of each of the five items in the scale

For each indicator, select the number from 1 to 5 that most accurately describes your own behavior on a day-to-day basis.

"One of the major obstacles to school improvement efforts is that teachers and administrators have perceived the instructional role primarily in terms of what one individual does with classes of students and there has been a much less clear picture of the role as a collaborative faculty member."

Bruce Joyce and
Beverly Showers

INSTRUCTIONAL LEADERSHIP
BEHAVIORAL CHECKLIST

STEP TWO: Be there for your staff.

Indicator 2.1 Works with teachers to improve the instructional program in their classrooms consistent with student needs

Comment:

The main focus of Indicator 2.1 is the role of the principal as an instructional resource person for teachers. Quality and quantity of assistance are to be considered as well as the frequency with which teachers call on the principal for assistance.

SCALE OF DESCRIPTORS:

1. Principal has no interaction with teachers regarding the instructional program in their classrooms. Principal has almost no understanding of instructional program. Teachers never ask for instructional assistance from the principal, preferring to deal with instructional matters independently.

2. Principal rarely assists teachers with instructional concerns but will attempt to assist a teacher if a specific, well-defined request is made. Principal has very sketchy knowledge and understanding of the instructional program. Few requests are made by teachers for assistance.

3. Principal works in a limited way with those few teachers who request help. Principal's knowledge of instructional strategies is basic, and outside resources are often needed to solve instructional problems.

4. Principal works with most teachers through coordination and delegation, showing a strong degree of expertise. Teachers frequently turn to the principal for assistance.

5. Principal works with all teachers on a continuing basis and is an important resource for instructional concerns. Interaction is frequently initiated by the principal, and teachers regularly turn to the principal for help, which they receive with a high level of expertise.

KEY POINTS IN DESCRIPTORS:

1. No interaction, no expertise, no requests for assistance

2. Little interaction, limited expertise, few requests for assistance

3. Some interaction, basic expertise, some requests for assistance

4. Frequent interaction, strong expertise, frequent requests for assistance

5. Regular interaction, outstanding expertise, regular requests for assistance

Indicator 2.2 Bases instructional program development on sound research and practice

Comment:

The main focus of Indicator 2.2 is the status of the principal as an active learner in the acquisition of current educational research and practice, and how effectively this knowledge base is shared and translated into instructional programs.

SCALE OF DESCRIPTORS:

1. Principal is unaware of current educational research and practice.

2. Principal is aware of current educational research and practice but feels this body of knowledge has little bearing on the day-to-day functioning of the school.

3. Principal is aware of current educational research and practice and believes it should affect program development but is not currently attempting to translate this information into practice.

4. Principal is aware of current educational research and practice, believes it should affect program development, shares it actively with staff, and is currently attempting to translate this information into instructional program development.

5. Principal is aware of current educational research and practice, believes it should affect program development, shares it actively with staff, and has successfully developed and/or altered school programs to reflect this knowledge base.

KEY POINTS IN DESCRIPTORS:

1. No awareness of or belief in the importance or use of current educational research

2. Some awareness of but no belief in importance or use of current educational research

3. Some awareness of and belief in importance but no use of current educational research

4. Awareness of and belief in importance and some attempts to translate information into instructional program

41

5 Awareness of and belief in importance; successful implementation of school programs based on research

Indicator 2.3 Applies appropriate formative procedures in evaluating the instructional program

Comment:

The main focus of Indicator 2.3 is the combination of multiple methods of evaluation that are formative in nature and allow for immediate adjustments in instructional strategies, groupings, time allocations, and lesson design.

Examples of formative evaluation tools are teacher-made tests, samples of student work, mastery skills checklists, criterion-referenced tests, end-of-unit tests, and so on.

SCALE OF DESCRIPTORS:

1. Principal does not receive any regular formative evaluation information from classroom teachers.

2. Principal receives some formative evaluation information from some classroom teachers, but sharing of this information is voluntary.

3. Principal solicits some formative evaluation information regularly from all classroom teachers.

4. Principal solicits some formative evaluation information regularly from all classroom teachers and discusses this information with teachers.

5. Principal solicits complete formative evaluation information regularly from all classroom teachers, discusses this information with teachers, and together with teachers plans for changes in day-to-day classroom practices.

KEY POINTS IN DESCRIPTORS:

1. No regular formative evaluation information

2. Some voluntary formative evaluation information

3. Formative evaluation information solicited regularly

4. Formative evaluation information solicited regularly and discussed

5. Formative evaluation information solicited regularly, discussed, and instructional practices adjusted

STEP THREE
Create a School Culture and Climate Conducive to Learning

How can you establish high expectations?

The goal of establishing high expectations is a worthy one, but how can it be translated into the day-to-day behavior in the principalship? Most of us feel we have high expectations, but what do they look like? If this phrase becomes the rationale for high failure rates, then we have not achieved our goal. Alan Jones stated it this way:

To foster academic achievement, schools need to do more than simply set demanding standards for children. They need to structure academic experiences in a way that enhances students' sense of academic efficacy. Good instruction helps students at all levels, regardless of teacher expectations.

Five primary ways in which effective instructional leaders communicate high expectations for the students of their schools are through:

1.	Establishing inclusive classrooms that send the message that all students can learn
2.	Providing extended learning opportunities for students who need them
3.	Observing and reinforcing positive teacher behaviors in the classroom that ensure an academically demanding climate and an orderly, well-managed classroom
4.	Sending messages to students in a variety of ways that they can succeed
5.	The establishment of policies on student progress relative to homework, grading, monitoring progress, remediation, reporting progress, and retention/promotion

Inclusive classrooms. The tracking of students of varying ability levels and the segregation of students with special needs send messages to these special populations and their parents that some students don't have what it takes to make it in the regular classroom. Over the years we have communicated to them that they need different teachers, different rooms, different textbooks, and a different set of expectations to succeed.

Instructional leaders have a big job ahead of them. Fortunately, many communities and districts are beginning to address these inequities. Linda Hanson's high-school district

44

is sending the message that all students, except those in a few honors courses, can learn through detracking. West Chicago, Illinois schools are including all of their students with special needs in the regular classrooms. There are no self-contained special education classes; rather, facilitating teachers and teacher assistants provide support to students with disabilities and their teachers. Research clearly documents the insidious effects of tracking on lower-achieving students. There are "clear differences between upper and lower tracks in regard to the content and quality of instruction, teacher-student and student-student relationships, the expectations of teachers for their students, the affective climate of classrooms, and other elements of the educational enterprise. It appears that those students for whom the most nurturant learning would appear to be appropriate received the least."[1] Effective instructional leaders are beginning to change the way teachers look at tracking and through careful planning with staff are restructuring their classrooms. A helpful checklist of assessing tracking practices in your school is provided by Eleanor Linn and Norma Barquet.[2] Among the forty questions they ask in areas such as staff expectations, student placement, and evaluation procedures are these:

> "Despite the fact that the assumption that students learn more or better in homogeneous groups is almost universally held, it is simply not true. Or, at least, we have virtually mountains of research evidence indicating that homogeneous grouping doesn't consistently help *anyone* learn better."
>
> Jeannie Oakes

> "Every school must believe that all children can learn and that all teachers and administrators can help them."
>
> William Gauthier, Jr.

1.	Has a survey of school culture or climate been undertaken to ensure that every student has the necessary personal and academic support to achieve the district's expectations?
2.	Are all students required to take more than two years of math and science at the high school level?
3.	Is the grouping of students for instructional purposes flexible, temporary, and intended to accelerate learning?

4.	Are critical thinking, expository writing, and oral presentations an integral part of all student programs?
5.	Is persistence taught, valued, and rewarded in all classes?
6.	Have students been followed after graduation to see what kinds of jobs and education they have pursued to determine the school's success in preparing students?
7.	Do staff members avoid using such terms as "bright students," "able learners," "college-bound," "remedial," "lower-track," and "LD" to refer to specific groups of students?
8.	Are girls, students with low socioeconomic status, minorities, students with physical disabilities, and limited-English-speaking students represented in leadership roles such as student council and student government?

Extended learning opportunities. Instructional leaders who have established outcomes for all students, and are committed to the belief that all children can learn, quickly realize the impossibility of attaining their goals if extended learning opportunities are not offered to the students who need them. In the words of Dr. William Spady, who has redefined for many instructional leaders what success for all really means, "The important thing is not 'when' a student learns something, but 'whether' a student learns something." Application of this commonsense principle, which Spady compares to the Girl and Boy Scout merit badge systems, an apprenticeship program, or simply receiving a license to drive a car or fly a plane, means that instructional leaders must find ways to break through the time barrier that keeps large numbers of students from mastering the outcomes we have so carefully developed in our committees and task forces.[3]

Teacher behaviors in the classroom. Research over an extensive period of time has shown that low-achieving students are treated differently by teachers than high-achieving students. Teachers give more praise and approval to high-achieving students than to low-achieving students.[4] Children perceived as low achievers received fewer reading turns, fewer opportunities to answer open or direct questions, and fewer opportunities to make recitations, and they were less apt to call out answers. Children perceived by the teacher as high achievers received more praise and less criticism than children perceived as low achievers.[5] Students from ethnic minorities are also often treated differently by teachers. Mexican American students in one study experienced more interaction with the teacher than Anglo students in only two areas—giving directions and criticizing. In all positive categories, the Anglo students experienced more interaction.[6]

> **"TRAVELIN' THE USA, HESTER INDUSTRIES' WAY!"**
>
> At the Moorefield Elementary School in Moorefield, West Virginia, they've found a unique way to team up with a business partner. Peggy Hawse and her staff work with a frozen chicken processing firm, Hester Industries. The Hester trucks travel all over the USA. The truck drivers, many of whom are Moorefield parents, take cameras with them and bring back pictures of historic sites and landmarks. The pictures are mounted on a huge map of America located near the entry of the school. A short description of each picture is attached, and a string indicates the exact location of the picture.

Reserachers have cited eighteen different variables of instruction between low-ability and high-ability students—for example, lower-ability students receive the least prepared teachers, are more likely to receive instruction from aides, and spend less time on interactive teaching and more with worksheets. They identify nine time variables that differ between low-ability and high-ability students—for example, lower-ability students lose more instructional time in transitions, spend more class time devoted to homework, and spend more time with no work assignments. Finally, they cite twenty-one different variables related to curriculum content—for example, content for low-ability students is less academically oriented, material is covered at a slower pace, and fewer tests are given. They also cite three different variables of success—for example, low-ability students engage in more off-task behavior and have lower rates of success.[7]

Instructional leaders have an obligation to observe carefully and monitor how teachers interact with both high-achieving and low-achieving students and to then provide training and assistance for teachers to help them change in the necessary areas. One powerful training program used by many instructional leaders is TESA (Teacher Expectations and Student Achievement).[8] The program consists of five mini-units in each of three strands that emphasize the concept of equity in educational opportunity: response opportunities, feedback, and personal regard. The lessons take participants through fifteen different ways in which teachers interact with students to raise expectations and thus achievement. Participants are encouraged to observe one another between each workshop session and collect data on their interactions with students. The units include information to assist teachers in learning how to

- Equitably distribute among students the opportunity to respond
- Affirm and correct appropriately a student's response
- Position oneself and move around the classroom appropriately so that all students have an awareness of the teacher's presence
- Provide help to low achievers as frequently as high achievers
- Praise the learning performance of lower achievers as frequently as that of other students
- Use courteous words as frequently with low achievers as with other students and as frequently with all students as with adults

---

BOOKS TOO GOOD TO MISS

In Wayland, Massachusetts, Richard Fitzpatrick has invited local "celebrities" to read selected stories over the local cable station. Tapes are broadcast regularly over cable and can be used at school as well.

- Give low achievers as much time to respond to a task or question as given to other students
- Tell low achievers as frequently as other students why their classwork is acceptable or praiseworthy
- Give personal compliments to low achievers as frequently as to other students and to express personal interest in the outside activities of low achievers as frequently as to other students
- Help all students respond to questions by providing additional information to them
- Listen attentively to low achievers as well as to other students
- Touch low achievers in a friendly manner as frequently as high achievers are touched in a friendly manner
- Challenge the thinking abilities of low achievers as often as other students by requiring them to do more than simply recall information
- Convey to all students that their feelings are understood and accepted in a nonjudgmental manner
- Be cool and calm when stopping the misbehavior of low achievers, just as with high achievers

"School climate starts at the curb."

Anonymous principal

Sending messages to students and teachers. Instructional leaders use a variety of techniques to keep students and teachers focused on the goal of learning for all. Sister Catherine Wingert uses community speakers throughout the year to relate the importance of high standards of work and act as role models for students. Other instructional leaders select school themes or mottos. "Be the best you can be" is the motto of James Simmons's school in Mountain Home, Arkansas. He even has the motto printed on his business card. Stella Loeb-Munson and her staff in East Cleveland, Ohio, have borrowed Jesse Jackson's motto—"Conceive it, believe it, achieve it."

Although instructional leaders focus a great deal of attention on academic achievement, they also recognize that every student cannot be at the top. Roger Moore and his staff in Lake City, Michigan, have Personal Growth assemblies every month. In these assemblies students are given awards for showing improvement. Parents are invited. Every student in the school receives at least one award each year. Diane Borgman and her staff in Soldotna, Alaska, have a "These Are Great Kids" board in the hallway. Teachers place certificates on the board for accomplishments of students in their classrooms. Every child receives recognition before a new cycle begins.

Establishing policies on student progress. Effective instructional leaders develop policies jointly with faculty members that address homework (Are assignments commensurate with grade levels and appropriate learning activities?); progress monitoring (Are parents notified immediately whenever a student is falling behind or having a problem?); remediation (Are there immediate steps to be taken when a student is in academic trouble or is he or she allowed to flounder for weeks?); progress reporting (Is there a system in place for reporting progress to parents?); and retention/promotion (Is there a policy that addresses the body of research showing the deleterious effects of retention on students?).

Effective instructional leaders make sure that none of the following practices decrease the odds for student success:

- Using varying grading scales
- Worshipping grade averages
- Using zeroes indiscriminately
- Following the assign/test/grade/teach pattern of instruction
- Not maintaining teaching/testing congruency

ACADEMIC BUDDY PROGRAM

At Niles North High School (Illinois) Tom Giles and his staff identified 25 to 40 of the academically neediest students and developed a support program for them. Each student was teamed up with an adult in the school (teacher, administrator, clerk, support staff) who helped the student develop the skills he or she needed to be more successful.

- Implying the deck is stacked against students
- Practicing "gotcha" teaching
- Grading first efforts
- Penalizing students for taking risks
- Establishing individual criteria
- Not providing an appeals process

Dr. John O'Connell of Prince George's County, Maryland, Public Schools uses the topic of grades to encourage teachers to examine expectations and how they relate to the teaching/learning and quality/equity issues.[9] You may wish to use his logic to engage your teachers as well.

IF: Teachers are teaching the curriculum, and

IF: Grades are a fair indication of whether students are learning that curriculum,

THEN: Grades can be used as a kind of Criterion-Referenced Testing (CRT)measure for teaching/learning.

IF: Grades can be used as a kind of CRT measure for teaching/learning, and

IF: Students are placed in groups (reading at the elementary school) or levels (secondary Basic English, Advanced English, Honors English) so that we can adjust instruction to meet their needs...so that students can be successful,

THEN: Grades can be used to determine whether instruction is being adjusted appropriately, whether students are being successful, and so on.

"It seems to me probable that the proportion of grammar school children incapable of pursuing geometry, algebra, and a foreign language would turn out to be much smaller than we now imagine."

Charles W. Eliot
(Committee of Ten, 1892)

How can you make sure time is being used effectively?

Increasing academic learning time is a critical task for the instructional leader. There are two ways to do this—make sure students are always in class and then make sure that when they're present, their time is being used for learning. Here are just a few of the ways effective instructional leaders go about improving student attendance:

- Read all of the student attendance policies provided by the board of education. Then make sure they are clearly communicated to staff, students, and parents. Develop a schoolwide plan on attendance, including reporting and follow-up. Consistency on the part of all staff members is crucial for success.

- Use an automatic dialing system with prerecorded messages to contact homes about student absences.

- Send a letter to parents at the beginning of the school year stressing the importance of attendance and requesting that vacations not be taken during the school year.

- Support teachers in improving classroom management. Provide recognition for teachers who motivate students and require punctuality. Require teachers to check attendance promptly every day. Encourage teachers to greet students personally every day. Refer habitual attendance problems to counselors or truancy programs.

- Be consistent in enforcing rules on attendance and tardiness. Require parental excuses for returning students, including medical excuses for extended absences. Hold personal conferences with students after extended absences. Encourage attendance competitions between classrooms. Don't suspend students from school for truancy or tardiness.

Getting students to school is only part of the "time-on-task" goal. Helping teachers focus on using that time efficiently and effectively is the second assignment for the instructional leader. The link between students being on task in the classroom and their academic achievement has been clearly established.[10] The instructional leader is constantly observing and taking note of the way all teachers use their time—not to play "gotcha" when students fail to measure up to expectations but to praise and reinforce the wise use of time. Instructional leaders pay special attention to the behaviors that characterize effective teachers and work tirelessly to increase the likelihood that all of the teachers in the building will fit these descriptors. They use verbal praise, short notes of commendation, and formal evaluation procedures to constantly remind faculty of the importance of the following behaviors that characterize effective teachers:

- Effective teachers spend at least half of their class time on interactive types of activities such as explaining new material, discussing and reviewing in small groups, hands-on activities, and project work.

- Effective teachers spend about one-third of class time on actively monitoring silent reading, written work, and lab work.

- Effective teachers rarely sit at their desks waiting for students to come to them. They move about the classroom on the lookout for students who need help, particularly those students who have been targeted by a child study team.

- Effective teachers spend less than fifteen percent of class time on classroom management and organization: passing paper, explaining activities, arranging desks, moving from one lesson to another, taking roll, making announcements, and so on.

- Effective teachers have a system of behavioral rules that are clear, posted in view, and consistently reinforced.

- Effective teachers spend very little time in class socializing with students, visitors, or aides.

- Effective teachers plan daily activities in advance and make them clear to students, for example, by writing the day's schedule on the board.

- Effective teachers plan a variety of academic activities using differing modalities during one class period.

- Effective teachers state the objectives and purpose of the lesson.

- Effective teachers give immediate feedback.

- Effective teachers focus most instruction on the whole class or small groups, rather than individuals.

- Effective teachers distribute opportunities for verbal response equally among students.

- Effective teachers praise student success and effort.

- Effective teachers give students who answer incorrectly another chance to get it right by rephrasing the question or giving hints.

- Effective teachers have an overview or review before presentation of new material and a summary and explanation at the end.[11]

What kinds of programs encourage students to learn?

Instructional leaders encourage programs and activities that motivate, make learning meaningful, and involve students in all aspects of school life. These activities are as varied as the schools, the children, the teachers, and principals. Meaningful instruction is the most important component of any program or activity, however. In Maryanne Friend's school, teachers believe that students learn best in "an atmosphere that treats learning as an exciting, dynamic activity. Teaching strategies are varied and motivating. A novel about a young boy living alone in the woods leads to a classroom lunch of 'woodsy' food items such as berries, apples, and nuts. A fifth-grade class studying American history is treated to vacation tapes from Williamsburg narrated by their teacher." Nick Friend agrees. He adds, "All programs and activities flow from our Effective School Plan. They include cultural assemblies, a dynamic intramural program that has a great deal of staff

A LEARNING CELEBRATION

The McPherson Middle School, where Merry Wade is the principal, celebrates learning in a yearly six-day event. A week before the event, personal invitations are sent to parents inviting them to attend. On Sunday a flashing portable sign is placed on the busiest street in town to invite the town's residents. On Monday students receive buttons reading "McPherson Middle School Celebrates Learning." Tuesday is Dress as Your Favorite Book Character day. Wednesday, there's a special assembly. Thursday is T-shirt day, and on Friday student awards are presented in twenty-five categories. Every student receives an award. To conclude, students form a circle and sing "The World Is a Circle." As students leave the gym, PTA members present them with red apples.

participation, Student of the Month selections, citizenship awards, student leadership program, clubs, sports, etc."

Many instructional leaders provide extended opportunities for students who need more time to learn. At McPherson Middle School, Merry Gayle Wade has study labs, math labs, and an after-school tutorial center. Teachers provide study times before and after school for students who need it. Students are encouraged to retake tests on which they have done poorly. Wade and her staff place importance on the actual learning, not on when it takes place. Lynn Sprick, a junior high school principal in Quincy, Illinois, provides support programs for students who need lots of follow-through and TLC, and an extended day for those needing a place to study, complete with resources and books. At Thornwood High School, Illinois, Gary Catalani and his staff provide a forty-minute communication period at the end of each day for tutoring.

Many instructional leaders plan reading incentive programs using both the Reading Is Fundamental program, which gives free books to students, and Chapter I's LIFT Program, which awards books to children who are working and improving. Other instructional leaders meet with small groups of students during lunch period to review for tests or do problem-solving activities.

Dave Burton relies on the 3 Fs—food, field trips, and friends—to motivate his junior high school students. Students are rewarded as much for effort as they are for achievement. Pizza, popcorn, and pop parties are frequent happenings. Trips to amusement parks, museums, skating rinks, and ski resorts are offered as rewards. Students enter into competitions such as Mathcounts, Science Olympiad, and Future Problem Solvers.

DINING OUT

The school lunch room/cafeteria at Harry Baldwin's school in Allenwood, New Jersey, is called a "dining room" and operated as though it were a restaurant. Round tables are covered with tablecloths, and silk flowers in milk glass vases are changed monthly. Guidelines developed by students for decorum and etiquette are printed and displayed in clear acrylic holders like those seen in restaurants. The result is a pleasant place to dine. Discipline problems are almost nonexistent.

Instructional leaders borrow ideas from others and adapt them to their own schools. They gather teachers, parents, and students together to brainstorm. Wherever and whenever there is a learning challenge, instructional leaders can find a way to overcome the hurdle.

Does your discipline support learning?

Good discipline in a school is a little like plumbing. When it is working, no one pays much attention to it. People just go about the important business of living and working and learning. When discipline or plumbing is broken, all meaningful activities cease until the problem is fixed. The existence of a safe and orderly climate appears on almost everyone's short list of what constitutes an effective school.

On discipline and safety, all the instructional leaders we interviewed agree. They believe that no student has the right to interfere with the learning of another student and unequivocally state they will not deny the opportunity for others to learn at the expense of an undisciplined child. Adamant about the importance of an environment that is safe and orderly enough for learning to take place, they believe that school must be a safe haven for learning. They recognize the importance of schoolwide rules and behavior management plans for each classroom. They also know that there is no *one* consequence or plan that works for all students and that sometimes consequences and plans need to be negotiated for individual students or problems. They focus on solving discipline problems in a way that is not punitive, yet they get the situation under control while opening the student's mind to the option of working in class. They are in frequent contact with parents, have teams in their building to solve problems when they arise, and often counsel with students individually. They use programs

---

ALTERNATIVE LEARNING DAY

Gary MacDonald is principal of the New Suncook School in Lovell, Maine. Each spring an Alternative Learning Day is organized by the PTA. There are nearly fifty different activities from which each student can choose. Children discover that learning can take place outside the classroom and share the joy of lifelong learning with community members.

such as Lee Canter's Assertive Discipline Program, or Curwin and Mendler's Discipline With Dignity. They constantly recognize students for good behavior with programs such as "Caught Being Good" and frequently try to avoid problems before they happen by instituting programs that pair students and staff members in mentoring or "significant other" relationships. Instructional leaders have outstanding discipline in their schools and believe there is no problem for which a solution does not lie just around the corner.

Lasley and Wayson have summarized these qualities.[12] The comments in italics are mine:

- All faculty members and students are involved in problem solving. *(Excluding anyone from the information and decision-making loop is bound to result in a pocket of resistance that can undermine any disciplinary structure.)*

- The school is viewed as a place to experience success. *(Mutual respect is the key to good discipline. If teachers and students continually play "gotcha" with each other, the system will break down.)*

- Problem solving focuses on causes rather than symptoms. *(What are the underlying causes that might be contributing to poor discipline—overcrowding, student frustration, punitive punishments?)*

- Emphasis is on positive behaviors and preventive measures. *(Be proactive rather than reactive.)*

- The principal is a strong leader. *(There is no individual that impacts the school atmosphere as much as the school principal. Everyone looks to the principal for direction and he or she must provide it in ways both tough and tender.)*

How can you alter culture and climate?

Culture is the way things are done in an organization, and climate is the way people feel about the culture. Culture and climate are feelings/beliefs/values that evolve over time. Do teachers in the building feel empowered? Do they believe that

> "Shared values define the fundamental character of their organization, the attitude that distinguishes it from all others. In this way, they create a sense of identity for those in the organization, making employees feel special."
>
> Terrence E. Deal and Allen A. Kennedy

> "A positive school climate is perhaps the single most important expression of educational leadership."
>
> Scott Thompson

all children can learn? Are problems typically solved through consensus and conflict resolution, or are they swept under the rug? Do people talk about "the good stuff" of education, or does the lounge talk center around picayune complaints? Climate has to do with the way people feel about the culture. Do people enjoy spending time with each other? Is the workplace a pleasant place to be?

Creating a school culture and climate that are conducive to learning is a challenging task for even the most effective instructional leader. But Terrence Deal has some suggestions that might prove helpful.[13]

First, he advises exploring and documenting a school's history. This exercise can be particularly helpful for the new principal who needs to know what values have evolved from the common experiences previously shared by staff, parents, and students. Deal then suggests that heroes and heroines be anointed and celebrated. In my former elementary principalship, we celebrated the retirements of teachers and staff members with a schoolwide assembly each year. Skits were performed, students gave testimonials, family members and former staff members were invited, and a reception complete with receiving line was held. A special plaque in the hallway contained the name and dates of service for all retired teachers. Students and staff were able to see the tangible rewards of a job well done. To celebrate our school's seventieth anniversary we invited all of the teachers still living who had retired from their teaching careers in our school. They shared anecdotes about their experiences and participated in the receiving line. Each year, we continued to anoint and celebrate heroes and heroines. This celebration is part of the culture of Lincoln School.

A third way of developing a culture to support learning is by reviewing the rituals. According to Deal, "living and meaningful rituals convey culture values and beliefs."[14] A ritual that characterized the opening of school each year for me as a building principal was the gathering on the playground of teachers, parents, and students. Each teacher carried a large sign mounted on a stick. On it was written his or her name, the grade level, and some suitable decorations. Students and parents consulted the class lists posted on the school doors and then found their teacher. Each teacher greeted his or her students personally, checking them off the list and warmly welcoming them to school. In my role as principal, I wandered about the playground greeting parents old and new, empathizing with those for whom the summer had seemed much too long, as well as with those who were reluctant to say goodbye to their children. After the bell rang and each class moved into the building, small groups of parents continued to talk. I circulated to each group, reestablishing old friendships and welcoming new faces. In the eight years we went through this opening day ritual, it never once rained. I had many contingency plans in my file, but fortunately our ritual went unchanged.

> **IT'S NOT BAD TO BE SMART**
>
> Richard Beck and his staff at the Stillman Valley High School (IL) have used the following ideas to cultivate and reinforce the attitude among students that it's not bad to be smart: They've developed an attendance incentive program, an academic trophy case, and an academic bulletin board; sent letters of congratulation to students and parents; put articles in the local paper; printed an awards recognition booklet; developed a scholarship medals program; increased the number of applications to academic competitions; given out award certificates; and held an academic awards banquet.

Ceremonies are another strategy for building school culture. Pep rallies, assemblies, sports contests, and graduation exercises are all ceremonies that can build school spirit. I recently witnessed such a ceremony in Joe Porto's school in Highland Park, Illinois. The pep assembly celebrated the essence of the school. Students were dressed in red and white, and each class had made up a cheer to show their pride in the school. From kindergarten to fifth grade, the cheers progressed in sophistication and complexity. They highlighted teachers, students, learning, and community. It was a remarkable event.

Remarkable in a different way was the pep assembly at a local high school that had won the state football championship. It provided a memorable ceremony for all the participants. Wearing new uniforms and carrying a new school name, the result of relocation to a larger facility, the team still retained its school mascot, a tiger. The tiger was the proud symbol of the past. As the principal, instructional leader Chuck Baker donned the tiger costume. Some might call this silly, but Chuck recognized and used that ceremony and symbolism to create yet another story for the school's rich history and tradition.

Storytelling is yet another way to build or revitalize a school culture. Tales of championship teams and remarkable performances can motivate both students and teachers to become part of a winning team. Teachers and principals can relive success stories with children. Remember how we taught Vicki to read in third grade when everyone had given up on her? This year she's captain of the Battle of the Books team. And remember the time the principal ran around the school in her bathing suit to spur us on to read more books? And who can forget when the custodian danced the polka with the principal at his retirement party? At Phyllis O'Connell's school, the stories that are retold relate to the "Fud Award." To be eligible for posting on the Fud Wall of Fame in the faculty lounge, a staff member must do something silly—like the one who drove through the car wash with her windows down because she was so preoccupied with a school problem. It's a dubious honor to be awarded a Fud, but there is a camaraderie amongst the award winners that makes new staff members almost wish to be a part of this "spacy" crew.

A final way to build culture is to encourage what Deal calls

PALS PROGRAM

At the Kingston Elementary School in Virginia Beach, Virginia, Lou Royal and her staff have organized Pupils Assisting Learning Service (PALS). Each morning from 8:30 to 9:00 a.m., students who need help with homework, test review, or any other skill reinforcement can work with another student in the cafeteria. The student helpers are trained by the guidance counselor to be helpful and positive when they work with their partners.

The students who need help improve significantly in the needed skills areas and their partners become more confident as they learn to help.

the network of priests or priestesses, gossips, storytellers, and other cultural players who keep the culture alive and intact. "Old practices and other losses need to be buried and commemorated. Meaningless practices and symbols need to be analyzed and revitalized. Emerging visions, dreams, and hopes need to be articulated and celebrated. These are the core tasks that will occupy educational leaders for several years to come."[15]

Another model of culture building is that of Saphier and King.[16] They hypothesize twelve norms of school culture that must be attended to in order for school improvement activities to have any effect. The norms include collegiality; experimentation; high expectations; trust and confidence; tangible supports; reaching out to the knowledge base; appreciation and recognition; caring, celebration, and humor; involvement in decision making; protection of what's important; traditions; and honest, open communication.

> "The ambience of each school differs. These differences appear to have more to do with the quality of life and indeed the quality of education in schools than do the explicit curriculum and the methods of teaching."
>
> John Goodlad

How can you use the Instructional Leadership Behavioral Checklist to assess your progress toward Step Three: Create a school culture and climate conducive to learning?

There are three indicators that describe Step Three in more detail:

1.	Establishes high expectations for student achievement that are directly communicated to students, teachers, and parents
2.	Establishes clear rules and expectations for the use of time allocated to instruction and monitors the effective use of classroom time
3.	Establishes, implements, and evaluates with teachers and students (as appropriate) procedures and codes for handling and correcting discipline problems

Every indicator is followed by three sections:

1.	A **comment** that defines the specifications of the indicator
2.	A **scale of descriptors** that gives a continuum of behaviors (1-5) from least effective to most effective
3.	**Key points** in the descriptors that give detailed explanations of each of the five items in the scale

For each indicator, select the number from 1 to 5 that most accurately describes your own behavior on a day-to-day basis.

INSTRUCTIONAL LEADERSHIP
BEHAVIORAL CHECKLIST

STEP THREE: Create a school culture and climate
conducive to learning.

Indicator 3.1 Establishes high expectations for student achievement that are directly communicated to students, teachers, and parents

---

Comment:

The main focus of Indicator 3.1 is the philosophical assumptions the individual makes about the ability of all students to learn, the need for both equity and excellence in the educational program, and the ability to communicate these beliefs to students, teachers, and parents.

SCALE OF DESCRIPTORS:

1. Principal believes that nonalterable variables such as home background, socioeconomic status, and ability level are the prime determinants of student achievement and that the school cannot overcome these factors.

2. Principal believes that the nonalterable variables cited above significantly affect student achievement and that the school has a limited impact on student achievement.

3. Principal believes that although the nonalterable variables cited above may influence student achievement, teachers are responsible for all students mastering basic skills/prescribed learner outcomes according to individual levels of expectancy. The principal occasionally communicates these expectations in an informal way to students, teachers, and parents via written and spoken communications and/or specific activities.

4. Principal believes that although the nonalterable variables cited above may influence student achievement, teachers are responsible for all students mastering certain basic skills at their grade level and frequently communicates these expectations to teachers, parents, and students in a formal, organized manner. Expectations for student achievement may be communicated through written statements of objectives in basic skills and/or a written statement of purpose/mission for the school that guides the instructional program.

5. Principal believes that together the home and school can have a profound influence on student achievement. Teachers are held responsible not only for all students

mastering certain basic skills at their grade level but for the stimulation, enrichment, and acceleration of the student who is able to learn more quickly and the provision of extended learning opportunities for students who may need more time for mastery. Expectations for student achievement are developed jointly among students, teachers, and parents, and they are communicated not only through written statements of learner outcomes in core curriculum areas but in enriched and accelerated programs, achievement awards, and opportunities for creative expression.

KEY POINTS IN DESCRIPTORS:

1. No impact by school on students; no communication of achievement expectations to students, teachers, or parents

2. Limited impact by school on students; no communication of achievement expectations to students, teachers, or parents

3. All students should master basic learner outcomes; limited communication of achievement expectations to students, teachers, and parents

4. All students should master basic learner outcomes; formal communication of achievement expectations to students, teachers, and parents

5. All students master basic learner outcomes with many students exceeding the minimal competencies, participating in enriched or accelerated course, and receiving academic awards; joint development of achievement expectations by students, teachers, and parents

Indicator 3.2 Establishes clear rules and expectations for the use of time allocated to instruction and monitors the effective use of classroom time

Comment:

The main focus of Indicator 3.2 is on the existence of written guidelines for the use of classroom time, the existence of a weekly program schedule for each classroom teacher, the regular monitoring of lesson plans, and the schoolwide schedule and its impact on instructional time.

SCALE OF DESCRIPTORS:

1. Teachers are totally unsupervised in the planning of their daily schedule. No written guidelines exist for the use of classroom time. There are frequent interruptions that significantly interfere with instruction.

2. State, district, or school guidelines for the use of classroom time exist, but the principal does not monitor their implementation in the classroom. There are many interruptions to instructional time that could be avoided.

3. State, district, or school guidelines for the use of classroom time exist, and the principal monitors their implementation in the classroom by requiring teachers to post a copy of their weekly schedule and by occasionally reviewing lesson plans. There are regular but infrequent interruptions on a planned basis.

4. State, district, or school guidelines for the use of classroom time exist, and the principal monitors their implementation by requiring teachers to post a weekly program schedule and regularly reviewing lesson plans. Basic skill instructional time is occasionally interrupted with advance notice. Whenever possible, interruptions are planned during noninstructional time.

5. State, district, or school guidelines for the use of classroom time exist, and the principal regularly monitors their implementation through the review of classroom or grade-level lesson plans and regular classroom visitations. Classroom instructional time is rarely interrupted, and the principal plans with teachers the coordination of schoolwide schedules to minimize the effect of pull-out programs, assemblies, and other special events.

KEY POINTS IN DESCRIPTORS:

1. No guidelines

2. Guidelines, no monitoring, frequent interruptions

3. Guidelines, limited monitoring, limited interruptions

4. Guidelines, frequent monitoring, few interruptions

5. Guidelines, frequent monitoring, coordinated school schedule to minimize interruptions

Indicator 3.3 Establishes, implements, and evaluates with teachers and students (as appropriate) procedures and codes for handling and correcting discipline problems

Comment:

The main focus in Indicator 3.3 is the existence of a discipline plan for each classroom and for the building as a whole, and the participation of the principal in the implementation of this plan. The focus of the plan is on responsible, caring behavior by all students and teachers based on mutual respect and common goals. Positive as well as negative reinforcers are included in the plan.

SCALE OF DESCRIPTORS:

1. Each classroom teacher has his or her own method of handling discipline problems without support or assistance from the principal, and there is no schoolwide discipline plan or comprehensive set of school rules.

2. Each classroom teacher has his or her own method of handling discipline, and no schoolwide discipline plan or set of school rules exists. The principal is available for assistance with severe discipline problems and handles them on an individual basis with little uniformity or consistency.

3. Each classroom teacher files a discipline plan with the principal, and rules for behavior in common areas of the building are available. The principal is generally supportive and provides assistance with discipline problems.

4. Each classroom teacher files a discipline plan with the principal. Rules for student behavior in common areas of the building have been developed jointly by the principal/ teachers/students (as appropriate) and made available to all parents and students. The principal is consistent and cooperative in implementing school discipline.

5. In addition to individual classroom discipline plans and rules for student behavior in common areas of the building, a buildingwide discipline plan has been developed in which the principal assumes a joint responsibility with all staff members, students, and parents for discipline and school behavior. A climate of mutual respect exists among students, teachers, and principal based on the fair application of the plan.

KEY POINTS IN DESCRIPTORS:

1. No classroom plans, no school rules, no schoolwide plan, no principal support

2. No classroom plans, no school rules, no schoolwide plan, some principal support

3. Classroom plans, school rules, no schoolwide plan, adequate principal support

4. Classroom plans, school rules developed jointly and furnished to students and parents, no schoolwide plan, and excellent principal support

5. Classroom plans, school rules developed jointly and furnished to students and parents, schoolwide plan developed jointly and furnished to students and parents, excellent principal support

Notes

1. Jeannie Oakes, *Keeping Track: How Schools Structure Inequality* (New Haven, Connecticut: Yale University Press, 1985), xi.

2. Eleanor Linn and Norma Barquet, "Assessing the Tracking Practices in Your School," *Equity Coalition, 12* (Ann Arbor, Michigan: Programs for Educational Opportunity, Autumn 1992): 16-17.

3. William Spady, from a presentation to the Suburban Superintendents Conference Traverse City, Michigan, (July 1992).

4. A. F. deGroat and G. G. Thompson, "A Study of the Distribution of Teacher Approval and Disapproval Among Sixth Grade Pupils," *Journal of Experimental Education, 18* (1949): 57-75.

5. Thomas L. Good and Jere E. Brophy, "Analyzing Classroom Interaction: A More Powerful Alternative," *Educational Technology* (1971): 36-41.

6. U.S. Commission on Civil Rights, *Teachers and Students: Differences in Teacher Interaction with Mexican American and Anglo Students*, Report V: Mexican American Education Study (Washington, D.C.: U.S. Government Printing Office, 1973).

7. James E. Rosenbaum, "Social Implications of Educational Grouping," in *Review of Research in Education,* David C. Berliner, ed. (American Educational Research Association, 1980), 361-401.

8. Phi Delta Kappa, *Teacher Expectations and Student Achievement* (Bloomington, Indiana: Phi Delta Kappa).

9. John O'Connell, from a presentation given at the National School Improvement Symposium, Farmington, Connecticut (1989).

10. B. Rosenshine and D. Berliner, "Academic Engaged Time," *British Journal of Teacher Education,* (1980): 3-16. B.S. Bloom, "The New Direction in Educational Research: Alterable Variables," *Phi Delta Kappan* (1980): 382-385. Jane Stallings, "Allocated Academic Learning Time Revisited, or Beyond Time on Task," *Educational Researcher* (1980): 11-16.

11. Jane Stallings, *Using Time Effectively in Classrooms,* paper presented at the National School Improvement Symposium, Farmington, Connecticut (1989).

12. Thomas J. Lasley and William W. Wayson, "Characteristics of Schools with Good Discipline," *Educational Leadership* (December 1982): 28-31.

13. Terrence Deal, "The Symbolism of Effective Schools," *The Elementary School Journal* (1985): 601-620.

14. Ibid., p. 616.

15. Terrence E. Deal, "The Culture of Schools," in *Leadership: Examining the Elusive,* Linda T. Sheive and Marian B. Schoenheit, eds. (Alexandria, Virginia: Association for Supervision and Curriculum Development, 1987), 14.

16. Jon Saphier and Matt King, "Good Seeds Grow in Strong Cultures," *Educational Leadership* (March 1985): 67-73.

CHAPTER FIVE

STEP FOUR
Communicate the Vision and Mission of Your School

What is the importance of vision and mission?

The literature often seems to use the terms *vision* and *mission* interchangeably, but to consider them as separate variables can help the instructional leader communicate both of them in more meaningful ways to staff, students, and parents.

I choose to define vision as "a driving force reflecting the instructional leader's image of the future, based on his or her values, beliefs, and experiences." Descriptors such as "universal," "immeasurable," "an object of the imagination," and "unusual discernment or foresight" come to mind. I believe vision is a personal view that provides the major direction an instructional leader will take. I define mission, on the other hand, as "the direction that emerges from the vision

69

and guides the day-to-day behavior of the organization." The mission, in order to be fully realized, must be developed collectively with your staff and community. Descriptors such as "measurable," "obtainable," "purposeful," "directional," "ultimate goal," and "commitment" come to mind when reflecting on the concept of mission.

When you as the instructional leader are hired for any new assignment, you will need a clear vision of what your school can become at some time in the future. You cannot be certain of the specific direction, or mission, that will emerge until you assess the school and community and work with the faculty. The vision is based on your values, your knowledge base, and your certainty that the future you envision will be far better than the school's present one.

In the beginning, any vision may be yours alone. At some point along the way, however, you will begin to share key ideas and concepts with faculty members, encourage them to read research and "think pieces" that expand their horizons, send them to conferences, and bring in outside speakers. You will talk about your values—what you believe to be important about teaching and learning. As the personal visions of your faculty begin to enlarge to encompass your vision, you will be ready to move to the next step—writing a building mission statement.

The mission statement will not be yours alone, however; it will be the school's. It will incorporate the collective visions of everyone and will be a consensus statement of where you want to go together. It will be attainable in the short term and will be measurable in some way. Out of the mission statement will flow goals, objectives, and action plans that will lead to the ultimate accomplishment of the mission. Phyllis O'Connell and her staff at Pioneer School have recently developed a second mission statement, believing they had achieved their first. It encompasses the views of every staff member as well as parents and students:

All children at Pioneer School will be actively engaged in meaningful learning experiences which will prepare them to be productive citizens in a global community. Students, parents, school personnel, community social services, and businesses will respectfully work together to share expertise, new ideas, experiences and talents so that authentic learning will occur. We seek to develop the whole person by addressing his/her individual needs, encouraging cooperation and celebrating diversity.

How can you develop communication channels?

Open door policy. Effective instructional leaders never, or rarely, close their doors. Even though they may be knee-deep in paperwork or problems, their body language says, "C'mon in. How can I help you?" Only salespersons need appointments with instructional leaders. All others are welcome at any time. Strong instructional leaders close their doors only when they are conferencing with students, parents, or teachers. They never close their doors to "work."

Arrive first; leave last. Effective instructional leaders seem to live in their school buildings. They are available both early and late to share concerns, laugh over a humorous happening during the school day, or brainstorm a solution to a problem.

Dialogue, dialogue, dialogue. There is no substitute for good conversation, and effective instructional leaders are constantly engaged in dialogue with teachers. When teachers aren't talking, instructional leaders are out and about, asking questions that will get the conversation flowing. They talk about research, teaching, learning, and finding new ways every day to make sure that teachers share the vision and mission of the school.

The grapevine. Every instructional leader has an informal communication network in place—an early

Mission starts with determining what you really care about and want to accomplish and committing yourself to it. You can always develop expertise. First, discover your preference."

Charles Garfield

warning system, if you will—that sends signals about major problems looming on the horizon. Often a well-placed word or action on the part of the instructional leader can head off these major problems.

Social events and TGIFs. Every instructional leader has his or her own philosophy about partying with the staff, but attending social events offers an opportunity to get to know staff outside of the school structure. Your ability to attend these events may be a function of the size of your school. The principal of a small elementary school will have far fewer invitations than the principal of a large high school with close to 150 staff members. I personally made an exception about attending weddings. It was well known among my staff that my husband hated weddings, and I made it a policy from the very beginning to send a generous gift and a warm letter. The policy was accepted because I was consistent in its implementation. Of the twenty-five to thirty weddings that took place during my principalship, I didn't go to one. Baby showers were a different matter, however. I was always there with another gift and played all of the games with gusto. Crashing "staff-only" parties is a no-no, of course. Don't nurse hurt feelings if you're not invited. Everyone needs to let their hair down once in awhile.

Visible presence in building. Research says that apart from what you say or do, or how you look or act, just being there has an enormous impact on how teachers and students conduct business in their classrooms. When you are out and about, you are communicating what is really important about the school, classrooms, and learning.

Weekly (daily) faculty bulletin. When I was a

GREAT EXPECTATIONS

Joseph Caruselle, principal of the Yekota East Elementary School on the Yekota Air Base in Tokyo, Japan, is exuberant in his approach to communicating his expectations to students. He schedules a thirty-minute session with each classroom teacher and his or her class within the first two weeks of school. Wearing his "Woody Woodpecker" or "Bullwinkle Moose" hat, he moves exuberantly around the room, encouraging the students to stand up and reach for the ceiling. "No," he tells them, "I mean really reach for the ceiling. Watch those arms stretch up. That's what Great Expectations are all about. Reaching higher than you thought you could."

building principal, this communication vehicle consistently got rave reviews. Each Monday morning, faculty received a communiqué with a calendar of weekly events, summaries of any important meetings that had been held the week before, information that was needed to get through the week, accolades for staff who had made contributions in the prior week, personal thoughts on teaching and learning from the principal, and a humorous note to keep us laughing.

Occasional lunches with teachers. I'm all in favor of putting in an occasional appearance in the teachers' lounge during lunch periods. Once a week is often enough, however. Again, as with parties, I believe staff members need thirty minutes to relax with their friends. The presence of the principal, albeit one with tremendous relationships with all staff members, nevertheless sets a different tone for the lunch period. Tom Giles, an outstanding high school principal, disagrees with me. He believes the faculty cafeteria is "the" place to eat.

CARVED IN STONE

Roger Moore of the Lake City Elementary School in Lake City, Michigan, has had his mission statement carved in stone by a local monument maker. It stands near the entrance to his school and reads: "Recognizing that we can all learn, the Lake City Area Community will provide a positive, academically sound learning environment by nurturing self-esteem and a lifelong love of learning."

Building leadership teams (curriculum council, management team). These small groups are invaluable as communications channels and decision-making vehicles for the building principal. They usually are organized in such a way that faculty members feel free to bring up any concerns, instructional or otherwise. The building team in turn discusses and makes recommendations back to the faculty. The instructional leader who has not had the opportunity to work with a team of teachers to implement school improvement initiatives has missed one of the most energizing experiences of the principalship. Instructional leadership can be shared, and teams of teachers are perfect places to begin the sharing. Make sure that minutes of team meetings are made available to all faculty. When it comes to the inside story, it's easy for the building team to become the "haves" and the rest of the staff the "have-nots."

Staff meetings. These meetings, held monthly or more often, are perfect vehicles for engaging in sharing sessions and group processes. Don't let your faculty meetings become boring recitations of management items that could easily be read in the faculty bulletin. Neither let them become vehicles for complaining and whining. Use them to do the important work of staff development, reach consensus on mission statements, discuss how to meet the needs of target students, iron out conflicts, and celebrate successes.

Team, department, or grade-level meetings. Meet with small groups on a regular basis. Be sure to take a yellow pad and pen with you. You will no doubt come away with several assignments and tasks. Your presence will energize and refocus those present, while your reiteration of the mission and vision of the school will encourage and renew them.

Surveys/force field analyses. You should never assume that no news is good news. Effective instructional leaders are constantly "dipsticking" the school community to make sure that everyone is focused on the goals. Simple surveys during the school year such as "What are we doing at XYZ School that we should keep doing?" and "What are we doing at XYZ School that isn't effective?" will send the message to your staff that you want to hear all of the news—not just the good stuff. The force field analysis is a helpful group-process technique to use if a problem looms large on the horizon. As you consider a goal or mission in the future, ask staff members to brainstorm all of the positive forces that will contribute to reaching that goal. Also ask participants to list all of the negative or restraining forces that are acting as barriers to achieving the goal. A process such as this can help identify communication or other types of barriers that are standing in your way. Many instructional leaders use a formal survey every three or four years to get a comprehensive look at how the system is functioning.

How can you communicate the value of learning?

Visible presence in classrooms, hallways, playground, lunchroom, bus stops, athletic events, extracurricular activities. Your visible presence with students is just as important as with teachers. Superprincipal has to be everywhere at once. You will communicate to students that they are important to you and you care about their learning, their behavior, and their lives.

Opportunities at all school assemblies to talk about learning. Effective instructional leaders never miss an opportunity to share an important idea or concept with students. Whenever students are gathered together for assemblies or special events, you will hear effective instructional leaders talking about the importance of achievement, the excitement of learning, the value of listening, or any of a dozen themes that run through principals' conversations with students.

All-school assembly at beginning of school year. Many instructional leaders kick off every school year with an assembly that sets the tone and focus for the year. Just as the opening institute day or faculty meeting is designed to set the course for the teachers, the all-school assembly sends the same message to students. It can include music, entertainment, a speech by the principal, or skits by teachers or students. Whatever the theme, it offers another opportunity to share the value and meaning of learning with students.

RALEIGH-BARTLETT MEADOWS INFORMATION CENTER

James Simmons, principal of the Nelson Wilks Elementary School in Mountain Home, Arkansas, and his staff established the "RBM" Information Center, a telephone number that enabled parents to keep in touch with their child's teacher twenty-four hours a day for verification of homework assignments, school activities, principal's messages, and school menus. The center also programmed calls to students' homes with positive messages from the principal and faculty.

Modeling a love of learning. Effective instructional leaders model a love of learning during every school day. They can be seen reading stories aloud in classrooms and libraries, curled up on a pillow in a classroom reading their favorite novel, writing in a journal with a group of high school students, or sharing slides from their vacation trip in a history class. They might use reference books and computers in the library or talk with students about how to design a certain lab experiment.

Smaller groups of students. Instructional leaders take advantage of small groups of students to communicate ideas and goals on a more personal basis. Some schools have Teacher Advisory Periods in which principals share ideas about test taking or social skills.

Written communication. Many instructional leaders have suggestion boxes where students can leave notes or large chart pads where students can write and principals can respond. Subjects range from the fare in the cafeteria to grades on the last social studies test.

Informal conversations/lunchroom discussions. Effective instructional leaders seek out informal conversations with students whenever possible. They are good communicators with students, in tune with the music, the books, the clothes, and the interests of any particular age group.

Academic communication. Good instructional leaders recognize their students' accomplishments. Commending students for outstanding achievement, listening to students read books aloud or share their writing, and sending personal notes to students who appear in newspaper articles are just some of the ways principals reinforce and commend learning.

POSITIVE BEGINNINGS

Two weeks before school begins, principal Evan Harrison of the Todd School in Roosevelt, Utah, sends a letter to every student. Each child is welcomed to school and invited to come and meet his or her teacher two days before school starts. The letter also gives pertinent information about the beginning of school. Evan goes to each classroom on the first day and while personally welcoming the students gives them a button. The messages are different each year—"I Love Todd School" or "We Have School

---

News articles. Effective instructional leaders never miss an opportunity to let the rest of the community know what is happening in their schools. They publish honor rolls, submit articles about special achievements, and feature students of the week and month in a special column.

Student council. Just as instructional leaders use Building Leadership Teams to establish solid two-way communications channels between faculty and principal, they use the Student Council as a way to build communication with students. Student Councils are marvelous vehicles for enlisting student support with spirit building and climate improvement. They can energize a student body to take on special causes such as building cleanup, recycling, or fund-raising for new library books.

School newspaper/magazine. A student-run newspaper or magazine is another important vehicle for determining what is important to students. Editorials and news articles should be carefully read and problems responded to with care and diplomacy.

Television. Many schools utilize the resources of in-house television to create their own school news broadcast each day. Instructional leaders frequently broadcast messages to students. Use these opportunities to "appear on TV" to reiterate the vision and mission of your school. Find new ways to communicate that mission in meaningful ways— through object lessons, humorous stories, or visuals.

Community resources. Graduates who talk about the importance of learning can have a powerful impact on students. We invited community members to our school to read aloud during a special week each year. But we also asked them to talk specifically about the importance of reading in

> **FAMILY PICNIC**
>
> Alan Stephenson of the Neal Dow Elementary School in Chico, California, starts the year with a picnic. His PTA organizes the event, which is held at a local park. Everyone brings food, but the PTA provides watermelon and organizes games.

> "Articulating a theme, reminding people of the theme, and helping people to apply the theme to interpret their work—all are major tasks of administrators."
>
> Karl Weick

their career. The fire chief brought in his manuals and policies. The electrician brought in his diagrams and schematics. The school superintendent even brought in his board policies and professional journals. It was another way to communicate the importance of learning to students.

How can you communicate with parents?

Classroom letters to parents. Encouraging each classroom teacher to write a weekly or monthly letter to parents is a powerful way to communicate with parents about what is happening at school. These letters can give ideas about activities for parents and students to do together.

Weekly (monthly) parent letter. Many instructional leaders write a weekly or monthly parent letter. It may or may not be part of a newsletter. It usually focuses on some aspect of learning and encourages parents to complete activities at home that support what the school is doing.

BROWN BAG LUNCH

Phyllis O'Connell of West Chicago, Illinois, holds Brown Bag Lunches with students. Community members or parents with interesting skills or careers are invited to share over lunch. Students might learn about flower arranging at one lunch and nuclear physics at the next. Students can choose which lunches they wish to attend.

Informal cottage coffees. Small groups of parents who gather in one individual's home for a morning or evening coffee can be a good communications channel. The principal and/or teachers attend to mingle informally with parents or possibly to make a brief presentation. These informal gatherings allow for different kinds of conversational exchanges than might occur in the more formal school setting. Some schools plan early breakfasts for moms and dads who work.

PTA/PTO/booster clubs. Every school needs a formal parent organization that allows all parents the opportunity to be involved at school in some way. Instructional leaders are skilled at working with these groups to achieve school goals, and they recognize the power that exists in an organized parent group. They meet with parents informally to plan agendas and set goals, and they attend all of the business meetings. The wise instructional leader uses the parent organization for more than just fundraising. He or she taps the collective wisdom of the group for accomplishing the school mission.

Homework hotlines. Many instructional leaders have found ways to use technology to communicate with parents. One of the most popular ways is a homework hotline. Parents can keep in touch with teachers and monitor their students' progress with only the press of a button. This program is very popular with parents.

Newspaper column. Writing a weekly newspaper column is another way that some instructional leaders communicate with parents. The column can feature school events, accomplishments of individual students, book reviews of outstanding reading for children, answers to questions that parents often ask, or advice about parenting issues. While the deadline of a weekly column is often a pressure for the busy instructional leader, the payback in terms of public relations and communication is incredible.

Family learning nights (afternoons). Invite parents to school to share learning experiences with children. Engage in hands-on science or math activities, dance the Virginia Reel in gym class, or do an art project together. These activities do more than just showcase your school; they model for parents how to learn with their children.

Back-to-school nights. These traditional open houses permit parents to "walk through" their child's school day, giving parents a feel for the teachers, the classrooms, and the expectations for their child. Open houses are important vehicles for communicating the mission of the

> **LESSON 'N' LUNCH**
>
> Francine Fernandez of Kailua, Hawaii, invites parents to participate in a classroom lesson just prior to the lunch period and then join their child for lunch. The Lesson 'n' Lunch happens twice a year with primary and upper-elementary students.

school to parents. Gathering parents together in one location prior to moving from classroom to classroom is a technique that many instructional leaders use. It is yet another opportunity to articulate for parents what "our school" is all about.

School newspaper. Student-produced newspapers are common at the high school level, but they can also serve as important channels of communication at the junior high and elementary levels. The school newspaper contains material written by and for students but is sent to parents and shows parents the quality of work that students are producing in the school.

School newsletter. This is an important communication vehicle at any grade level, but especially important at the junior high and high school levels, when parent involvement and interest may fall off sharply. The newsletter can contain schedules of special events, news of students' achievements, articles about new curricular offerings, and a special column or letter of greeting from the principal.

TAKE A MORNING WALK

Harvey Alvy at the American Embassy School in New Delhi has his secretary block out the first hour of every day so he can walk around the school and visit each classroom. He says hello to students and teachers and lets everyone know that the classroom is the center of the school, not the principal's office.

Parent-teacher conferences. These yearly or twice-yearly events are one of the most important communications events between parent and school. The focus is on the individual child and his or her needs, strengths, and academic progress. Instructional leaders spend time in helping all teachers structure effective conferences but focus particularly on new staff members.

Informal visits to homes. Home visits are time consuming, but they can be extraordinarily beneficial for building rapport and strong relationships between the home and school. While many districts use parent facilitators in preschool programs, home visits in upper grades are not as common as they used to be. Instructional leaders who are able to include them in their repertoire of communications channels are enthusiastic about the benefits.

How can you use the Instructional Leadership Behavioral Checklist to assess your progress toward Step Four: Communicate the vision and mission of your school to students, staff, and parents?

There are three indicators that describe Step Four in more detail:

1.	Provides for systematic two-way communication with staff regarding the ongoing objectives and goals of the school
2.	Establishes, supports, and implements activities that communicate to students the value and meaning of learning
3.	Develops and utilizes communications channels with parents for the purpose of setting forth school objectives

Every indicator is followed by three sections:

1.	A **comment** that defines the specifications of the indicator
2.	A **scale of descriptors** that gives a continuum of behaviors (1-5) from least effective to most effective
3.	**Key points in the descriptors** that give detailed explanations of each of the five items in the scale

For each indicator, select the number from 1 to 5 that most accurately describes your own behavior on a day-to-day basis.

INSTRUCTIONAL LEADERSHIP
BEHAVIORAL CHECKLIST

STEP FOUR: Communicate the vision and mission of your school to students, staff, and parents.

Indicator 4.1 Provides for systematic two-way communication with staff regarding the ongoing objectives and goals of the school

Comment:

The main focus of Indicator 4.1 is the provision of two-way communications channels to ensure an ongoing discussion of the mission of the school.

SCALE OF DESCRIPTORS:

1. There is no communication between principal and staff regarding the mission of the school.

2. Communication between principal and staff is largely one-way and limited to administrative directives regarding principal expectations.

3. Although principal and staff communicate informally regarding the mission of the school, there are no regular two-way communications channels.

4. Two-way communications channels between principal and staff have been established in the form of faculty meetings, grade-level/departmental/team meetings, and teacher/principal conferences, but these channels are frequently used for administrative or social purposes and are not regularly devoted to a discussion of instructional goals and priorities.

5. Established two-way communications channels are regularly used by the principal as a means of conveying the goals and objectives of the school to the staff.

KEY POINTS IN DESCRIPTORS:

1. No communication

2. One-way communication, no established channels

3. Informal two-way communication, no established channels

4. Established channels, no regular use of these channels

5. Regular use of established channels for two-way communication regarding school mission

---

Comment:

The main focus of Indicator 4.2 is the existence of activities that communicate the value of learning to students. Examples of such activities might be awards or honors assemblies, learning incentive programs, career awareness programs, honor societies, work/study programs, academic clubs, and mentoring or shadowing programs. This list is meant to be prescriptive but certainly not inclusive.

SCALE OF DESCRIPTORS:

1. No activities exist that communicate the value and meaning of learning to students.

2. At least one activity exists that communicates the value and meaning of learning to students.

3. More than three activities exist that communicate the value and meaning of learning to students.

4. More than six activities exist that communicate the value and meaning of learning to students.

5. More than ten activities exist that communicate the value and meaning of learning to students.

KEY POINTS IN DESCRIPTORS:

1. No activities

2. One activity

3. More than three activities

4. More than six activities

5. More than ten activities

Indicator 4.3 Develops and utilizes communications channels with parents for the purpose of setting forth school objectives

Comment:

The main focus of Indicator 4.3 is the existence of communications channels that are specifically devoted to setting forth school objectives to parents. Examples of communications channels might include but are not necessarily be limited to grade-level curriculum nights, newsletter columns devoted specifically to school objectives, parent conferences, written statements of school mission, written statements of instructional objectives for each grade level in each basic skill area, and school activities devoted to skill mastery that require parent participation and/or homework policy.

SCALE OF DESCRIPTORS:

1. No communications channels exist for the purpose of setting forth school objectives.

2. At least three communications channels exist for the purpose of setting forth school objectives.

3. At least six communications channels exist for the purpose of setting forth school objectives.

4. At least ten communications channels exist for the purpose of setting forth school objectives.

5. In addition to the ten communications channels that exist for the purpose of setting forth school objectives, the principal and faculty evaluate, refine, and develop additional means of communicating with parents regarding school objectives.

KEY POINTS IN DESCRIPTORS:

1. No channels

2. At least three channels

3. At least six channels

4. At least ten channels

5. At least ten channels and an evaluation, refinement, and developmental process

CHAPTER SIX

STEP FIVE
Set High
Expectations for
Your Staff

How can you set high expectations?

Setting high expectations for teachers is similar to setting them for students. You describe a standard of excellence and benchmarks of achievement and then do everything you can to help teachers meet that standard and reach those benchmarks. The same tensions that exist in setting high expectations for students plague instructional leaders as they work with teachers. How can you provide outstanding clinical supervision and coaching in an environment that calls for strict evaluation and assessment? How can you work collegially with teachers within the context of a negotiated contract? Somehow, effective instructional leaders are able to manage this high-wire act, and they have learned to move artfully between supervision and evaluation, letting teachers know they believe in them and that they will help them reach their personal and professional goals.

How can you assist teachers in setting goals?

Assisting teachers in setting personal and professional goals is part of what Jon Saphier calls "infusing the knowledge base about teaching into the life of the school." Helping teachers set personal and professional goals is a tricky task for instructional leaders, however. A staff of thirty may have beginners and veterans, subject-matter specialists and generalists, and right-brained and left-brained learners. Instructional leaders must be flexible enough to match the personal and professional goals to the individual teacher and skillful enough to bring the best out of everyone. Chris Gaylord is particularly effective in this area. She helps each teacher individually tailor his or her goals based on talent, commitment, and the reality of the life situation of each.

Sister Catherine Wingert helps her teachers tie their personal goals to the building goals, thus avoiding fragmentation and lack of focus, while Paul Zaander asks his staff to develop goals that relate to instructional improvement in both their classrooms and the school community. Effective instructional leaders publicly share their own personal goals with the staff. This public "baring of the soul" serves two purposes: (1) It holds the administrator accountable before his or her staff for accomplishment of the goal and (2) it offers a positive role model for risk taking and self-improvement.

Stella Loeb-Munson encourages her teachers to set professional goals beyond the classroom. She focuses on presentation skills and showcasing expertise in contests and award competitions. Linda Hanson encourages teachers to write books and do original research. Whatever the goal,

"Several images come to mind when thinking about those occasions when the principal is in direct contact with a teacher or teachers with regard to the instructional process: the captain with sword drawn, leading the charge; the coach in the huddle during a timeout diagramming a play; the sales manager giving a pep talk; the orchestra director conducting a rehearsal."

Keith Acheson

following up on its accomplishment is critical if the process is to have meaning and credibility. Most instructional leaders meet several times per year with each teacher to receive an update on goal progress. As the year draws to a close, progress is summarized and goals for the following year are discussed.

Critical to any self-improvement effort that teachers undertake, however, is their willingness to make changes within themselves. Change imposed from the outside is rarely meaningful. When staff members observe the instructional leader setting goals and changing behaviors (e.g,. setting goals to be a more visible presence in the building and to increase the number of class-rooms visited each day and accomplishing both), the goal-setting process will have more meaning and relevance to them. Actions always are more impressive and long-lasting than verbiage.

> "The individual has within himself vast resources for self-understanding, for altering his self-concept, his attitudes, and his self-directed behavior.... These resources can be tapped only [if] a definable climate of facilitative psychological attitudes can be provided."
>
> Carl Rogers

Where can you find time for observations?

The question of how principals spend their time is a function of what they're expected to do as well as what tasks and responsibilities they value most. Krajewski found in 1978 that principals placed the highest value on instructional leadership activities and the lowest value on tasks in the management area. However, when their values were compared to the way they actually spent their time, there was a large discrepancy.[1] More recent research by Smith and Andrews compared the way average instructional leaders versus strong instructional leaders spent their time as perceived by their respective teaching staffs.[2] Average principals believed they *should* allocate the greatest percentage of time to educational program improvement, but in reality they spent far more time on management and student services. Strong instructional leaders, however, accomplished the management tasks in a time frame similar to the average instructional leaders but spent far less time on student management issues like discipline. They have structures and systems in place that allow them to spend time more productively. Strong instructional leaders value educational improvement activities, manage their time wisely to accomplish these tasks, and still find time to get everything else done as well.

How do they find the time? "I don't find the time—I make time! Each month on my desk calendar I pencil in teachers/classes to observe, usually two per day," states Dave Burton, principal of West Chicago Junior High School in West Chicago, Illinois. Effective instructional leaders make classroom visits and observations an absolute priority. Says Nick Friend, principal of the A. Vito Martinez Middle School in Shorewood, Illinois, "I do not schedule anything during the school day that can be held before or after school, in order to make classroom visits my priority." They are adamant about the need to allocate time, especially Alan Jones, principal of West Chicago Community High School, a Blue Ribbon Award of Excellence School. "You must place your observations on your calendar, and treat them the same way you'd treat an appointment with your superintendent." Mike Klopfenstein, principal of Pine Bluffs Elementary School in Pine Bluffs, Wyoming, put it this way, "I schedule the observations and ask my secretary not to interrupt for anything short of someone dying."

Instructional leaders use a variety of techniques to keep organized. Some keep clipboards or journals. Some put their observations on the calendar during the month of August and work everything else around them, rather than making the observations fit in. They communicate to everyone—secretaries, teachers, parents, and even the superintendent—that classroom observations are a priority and will not be interrupted.

INNOVATIONS THE EASY WAY

At Pine Bluffs Elementary School (Wyoming), Mike Klopfenstein offers his teachers an alternative to the regularly scheduled evaluation (every third or fourth year). They can do a project for the year instead of going through the formal evaluation procedure. At the close of the year, the teacher is asked to present his or her project to the rest of the faculty. Among the projects teachers have tried are literature-based reading instruction, cooperative learning, outcomes-based education, and computer literacy.

How can observation and feedback be used to improve performance?

The types of observation and data-collecting procedures principals use are often mandated by the settings in which they work. The instruments, the methodologies, the length of observations, and the frequency of pre- and postconferences are usually dictated by the negotiated contract and/or district policies. Regardless of the methodologies they use, however, instructional leaders are in almost universal agreement that observation and feedback are near the top of the list for improving instruction.[3] Unfortunately, this is not how many principals spend their time.[4] If principals believe that observation and feedback are critical, why don't they do it more regularly?

- Quality teacher observations are time consuming.

- Quality teacher observations require confidence in one's own knowledge and skills.

- Providing quality feedback, especially in the context of teacher evaluation, is difficult and stressful for both the teacher and the principal.

> **VIDEO EVALUATION**
>
> Phyllis O'Connell varies her evaluation techniques. Rather than personally going to the classroom, she encourages teachers to videotape their lessons. Then she and the teacher conference together as they watch the tape.

Conducting high-level observations and structuring meaningful feedback sessions are comparable to the activities of working out and eating healthily. We all know how good the latter are for us, but they require discipline, structure, organization, commitment, skill, and some sacrifice. Similarly, we all know how beneficial observation and feedback are to the improvement of instruction, but they also require discipline, structure, organization, commitment, skill, and some sacrifice.

There are several knowledge and skill areas that are essential for the effective instructional leader:

- Knowledge about instructional strategies, subject matter, as well as the personality and characteristics of the teacher[5]
- Access to a variety of data collection devices and skill in recording data
- Recognition of appropriate goals and outcomes for individual teachers
- The ability to give helpful and collegial feedback

Intense concentration, penetrating analytical skills, and the ability to capture both minute detail and the big picture in a written form are only a few of the requirements for Superprincipal. Once data has been observed, collected, and analyzed, the task has only just begun. The most crucial aspect of teacher observation/evaluation is the sharing of feedback in a collegial manner that facilitates open discussion and leads the teacher to reflect on his or her teaching. Bird and Little call this "reciprocity," and they offer a five-point standard for principal/teachers to follow to ensure that observations result in the improvement of instruction and hence increased learning by students:[6]

- The principal must promise to bring knowledge and skill to the observation in order to help the teacher.

- The teacher must acknowledge that he or she has something to learn from hearing the principal discuss his or her teaching.

- The principal must demonstrate a certain level of skill and knowledge so as to give credibility to his or her statements about the teacher's performance.

- The principal must be able to provide the teacher with one or more of the following: some type of detailed recording of the observation, such as a coded chart or a script-tape; an idea or suggestion of some alternative practice that would be more effective than what the teacher is doing; a detailed description about what is outstanding in the lesson; and in some cases, a personally taught lesson so the teacher can observe the principal.

- The teacher must try to change his or her teaching practices in response to the observation/evaluation.
- The principal has an obligation to improve along with the teachers in training, practice, and observation of the interactions with teachers.

Perhaps a concrete example will more clearly illuminate the meaning of reciprocity. As a beginning principal, I was eager to acquire skills in observing and conferencing. I went to workshops, enrolled in administrators' academies, and practiced. The district in which I worked hired a consultant to provide assistance in clinical supervision for anyone who was interested, and I eagerly volunteered. The consultant and I observed a lesson together. The consultant then observed me conferencing with that teacher. We worked from a shared knowledge base about what had happened during the lesson. The consultant then conferenced with me regarding my conference with the teacher. This was such a successful experience, I invited several brave teachers to try other variations with me. I taught a lesson, and one of my teachers observed and conferenced with me. One of my teachers and I observed a lesson together, and she observed me conferencing with the teacher and gave me feedback. Then, in a moment of insane risk taking, I volunteered myself and a staff member for the ultimate in public display of teaching and conferencing. We bused an entire class of sixth graders and their teacher to a local university where over one hundred principals observed the teacher conducting a math lesson. The principals recorded their data and personally evaluated the lesson. I then participated in a panel with several other principals to talk about how we would have conferenced with the teacher. Reciprocity simply means remaining vulnerable and open to taking risks as an individual;

SELF-SERVICE

To reduce the stress of the formal observation and evaluation period, allow teachers to select the day and time of the principal's visit. Myra Spriggs at the Garnet C. Wilkinson Primary School in Washington, D.C., posts a calendar and permits teachers to sign up. In this way, she feels, teachers can be at their peak performance. This approach increases the comfort level of the observation and also tends to strengthen demonstrated skills.

it means that you, the principal, will never forget how personal the act of teaching often is, and that you will continually grow and change yourself as a professional.

What are the best conferencing techniques?

Effective instructional leaders spend a great deal of time and energy on observations and conferences. Merry Gayle Wade describes the process she uses:

> *I have an observational conference after each of my classroom visits. Before I go into the classroom, I decide what the focus of the visit will be. I take careful notes and write only what I saw, not what I think should have happened. After returning from the observation, I take a little time to review my notes and decide what I can share with the teacher to help him or her become more effective. I begin each conference by letting the teachers know I always enjoy visiting their class and ask how they felt about the lesson. This usually gets me in the improvement mode. When the teacher leaves my office I hope I have given them at least one idea they can use to improve their instruction. I believe teachers really want their administrators to know what they're doing. They want to be recognized for the difficult job they do. I see myself as a coach trying to lead the team into a winning year.*

Stella Loeb-Munson focuses every conference on the instructional process with one goal in mind—improvement of instruction. She asks these questions in every conference and although the questions remain the same, the solutions vary:

- Were the best of all possible choices for instruction in evidence?

- Were learning principles addressed and served to the benefit of every student?

- Did the students become involved and enthusiastic about their own learning?

- Did the goals set for the lesson happen? Why? Why not?

- How can we make this better?

- What do we add, take out, modify?

- What did you like best?
- What would you change? Why?

What is the importance of direct teaching?

Effective instructional leaders recognize the importance of engaging in direct teaching themselves. They feel that teaching in the classroom gives them an opportunity to show staff and students that they are teachers first and principals second. "I love the excitement generated by human beings learning and enjoying the process while they're doing it," said one. Another shared, "It gives principals an opportunity to model what they preach. It shows teachers that you are still a teacher and shows the students that you can still 'do it.'" Gary Catalani uses his teaching as a reward in a monthly drawing he holds with teachers. Two teachers receive a half-day release time. Gary teaches these classes while the teachers engage in professional activities.

How can you use the Instructional Leadership Behavioral Checklist to assess your progress toward Step Five: Set high expectations for your staff?

There are six indicators that describe Step Five in more detail:

1.	Assists teachers in setting and reaching personal and professional goals related to the improvement of school instruction and monitors the successful completion of these goals
2.	Makes regular classroom observations in all classrooms, both informal and formal
3.	Engages in preplanning of classroom observations
4.	Engages in postobservation conferences that focus on the improvement of instruction

5.	Provides thorough, defensible, and insightful evaluations, making recommendations for personal and professional growth goals according to individual needs
6.	Engages in direct teaching in the classroom of his or her school

Every indicator is followed by three sections:

1.	A **comment** that defines the specifications of the indicator
2.	A **scale of descriptors** that gives a continuum of behaviors (1-5) from least effective to most effective
3.	**Key points in the descriptors** that give detailed explanations of each of the five items in the scale

For each indicator, select the number from 1 to 5 that most accurately describes your own behavior on a day-to-day basis.

INSTRUCTIONAL LEADERSHIP BEHAVIORAL CHECKLIST

STEP FIVE: Set high expectations for your staff.

Indicator 5.1 Assists teachers in setting and reaching personal and professional goals related to the improvement of school instruction and monitors the successful completion of these goals

Comment:

The main focus of Indicator 5.1 is the active participation of the principal in the goal-setting process with teachers. Assistance is provided by the principal to the teachers in reaching stated goals, and the information obtained in the goal-setting process is utilized in teacher evaluation.

SCALE OF DESCRIPTORS:

1. Principal does not require that teachers set personal and professional goals.

2. Principal requires that teachers set personal and professional goals but is not involved in the goal-setting process and does not require that goals be related to the improvement of instruction.

3. Principal requires that teachers set personal and professional goals and that goals be related to the improvement of instruction but does not assist in the attainment of goals or monitor completion.

4. Principal requires that teachers set personal and professional goals in a cooperative way, insists that these goals be related to the improvement of instruction, and provides assistance in the attainment of these goals.

5. Principal requires that all teachers develop personal and professional goals related to the improvement of instruction in cooperation with the principal. Principal provides assistance to the teacher in the attainment of goals, monitors the completion of the goals, and utilizes the information in the evaluation process.

KEY POINTS IN DESCRIPTORS:

1. No goal setting by teachers

2. Goal setting not necessarily related to the improvement of instruction; no principal input, assistance, monitoring, or evaluation

3. Goal setting related to improvement of instruction; principal input; no principal assistance, monitoring, or evaluation

4. Goal setting related to improvement of instruction; principal input and assistance; no principal monitoring or evaluation

5. Goal setting related to improvement of instruction; principal input, assistance, monitoring, and evaluation

Indicator 5.2 Makes regular classroom observations in all classrooms, both informal (drop-in visits of varying length with no written or verbal feedback to teacher) and formal (visits where observation data is recorded and communicated to teacher)

Comment:

The main focus of Indicator 5.2 is on the quantity of classroom observations (both formal and informal).

SCALE OF DESCRIPTORS:

1. Principal makes formal classroom observations once every two years or less and never visits the classroom informally.

2. Principal makes at least one formal classroom observation per year and occasionally drops in informally.

3. Principal makes two formal classroom observations per year and at least one monthly informal observation.

4. Principal makes three formal classroom observations per year and at least two monthly informal observations.

5. Principal makes four or more classroom observations per year and visits the classroom informally at least once each week.

KEY POINTS IN DESCRIPTORS:

1. Minimal formal observations and no informal observations

2. One yearly formal observation and minimal informal observations

3. Two yearly formal observations and two monthly informal observations

4. Three yearly formal observations and two monthly informal observations

5. Four yearly formal observations and weekly informal observations

Indicator 5.3 Engages in preplanning of classroom observations

Comment:

The main focus of Indicator 5.3 is the quality of pre-planning prior to a formal classroom observation where information is being collected relative to improvement of instruction.

SCALE OF DESCRIPTORS:

1. There is no typical pattern. Principal stops in to visit in no systematic fashion. Teachers are not usually aware that the principal will visit.

2. Principal generally informs teachers before an observation. A lesson may be observed, but there is no specific request for such on the part of the principal.

3. Principal and teacher arrange together for a specific observation time. A complete lesson is usually observed.

4. Principal and teacher arrange together for a specific observation time. A discussion is held regarding the lesson plan for the observation, but no attempts are ever made by the principal to focus on specific curricular areas or instructional strategies (e.g., cooperative grouping in a reading lesson or questioning techniques used on target students). A complete lesson is always observed.

5. Principal and teacher plan the focus of each observation at a preconference. Principal frequently takes the initiative regarding the focus of the observation and relates it to building goals and objectives. A specific observation time is scheduled. A complete lesson is always observed.

KEY POINTS IN DESCRIPTORS:

1. No teacher awareness of observation; no preplanning conference; random observation of incomplete lessons

2. Teacher awareness of observation; no preplanning conference; observation includes both complete and incomplete lessons

3. Teacher awareness of observation; no preplanning conference; observation always includes complete lesson

4. Teacher awareness of observation; preplanning conference without specific focus by principal; complete lesson always observed

5. Teacher awareness of observation; preplanning conference with frequent principal initiative regarding subject of observation; complete lesson always observed

Indicator 5.4 Engages in postobservation conferences that focus on the improvement of instruction (District requirements for frequency and procedures with regard to teacher evaluation may vary and substantially impact the interpretation of this indicator. The scale of descriptors describes a best-case scenario.)

Comment:

The main focus of Indicator 5.4 is the quantity and quality of postobservation conferences that focus on the improvement of instruction.

1. Principal engages in a postobservation conference once every two years or less with each teacher, with little or no focus on the improvement of instruction.

2. Principal engages in one postobservation conference with each teacher every year but rarely focuses on the improvement of instruction.

3. Principal engages in two postobservation conferences with each teacher every year and provides one-way information about the improvement of instruction.

4. Principal engages in three postobservation conferences with each teacher every year, engaging in both one-way and two-way communication about the improvement of instruction.

5. Principal engages in four postobservation conferences with each teacher every year, engaging in both one-way and two-way communication about the improvement of instruction. Joint plans for follow-up in the classroom are developed with the principal providing instructional resources and assistance.

KEY POINTS IN DESCRIPTORS:

1. One conference every two years with no focus on improvement of instruction

2. One conference every year with rare focus on improvement of instruction

3. Two conferences every year with one-way communication about improvement of instruction

4. Three conferences every year with both one-way and two-way communication about the improvement of instruction

5. Four conferences every year with both one-way and two-way communication about the improvement of instruction; joint plans for follow-up with instructional resources and assistance provided

Indicator 5.5 Provides thorough, defensible, and insightful evaluations, making recommendations for personal and professional growth goals according to individual needs

Comment:

The main focus of Indicator 5.5 is the quality of the evaluation provided by the principal.

SCALE OF DESCRIPTORS:

1. All teachers receive nearly identical written evaluation ratings from the principal. There is no indication that evaluation is based on direct observation or supporting evidence, and no suggestions for improvement or growth are made.

2. Most teachers receive nearly identical written evaluation ratings from the principal. There is little indication that evaluation is based on direct observation or supporting evidence, and no suggestions for improvement or growth are made.

3. Although gradations of written evaluation ratings exist, these gradations appear to have no relationship to teacher performance or supporting evidence. No suggestions for improvement or growth are made.

4. Most teachers receive thorough written evaluations based on direct observation and supporting evidence. Principal makes few suggestions for improvement and growth.

5. Each teacher receives a thoughtful, written evaluation based on direct observation and supporting evidence. Principal includes suggestions for improvement and growth tailored to individual needs.

KEY POINTS IN DESCRIPTORS:

1. Uniform evaluations for all teachers, no supporting evidence, no suggestions for growth

2. Nearly uniform evaluations for all teachers, no supporting evidence, no suggestions for growth

3. Gradation of evaluation ratings, no supporting evidence, no suggestions for growth

4. Thorough evaluations for all teachers, supporting evidence, no suggestions for growth

5. Thorough evaluations for all teachers, supporting evidence, suggestions for growth

Indicator 5.6 Engages in direct teaching in the classrooms of his or her school

Comment:

The main focus of Indicator 5.6 is the number of times the principal teaches a lesson observed by the classroom teacher in his or her school. This indicator does not include reading stories aloud or assisting teachers. It focuses on lesson preparation and the opportunity for the classroom teacher to engage in an observation of this lesson.

SCALE OF DESCRIPTORS:

1. Principal engages in no direct teaching in the classroom.

2. Principal engages in direct teaching in any classroom at least once per year.

3. Principal engages in direct teaching in any classroom at least two to four times per year.

4. Principal engages in direct teaching in any classroom at least five to ten times per year.

5. Principal engages in direct teaching in the classroom more than ten times per year.

KEY POINTS IN DESCRIPTORS:

1. No direct teaching

2. One episode of direct teaching

3. Two to four episodes of direct teaching

4. Five to ten episodes of direct teaching

5. More than ten episodes of direct teaching

Notes

1. R. J. Krajewski, "Secondary Principals Want to Be Instructional Leaders," *Phi Delta Kappan* (September 1978): 65-69.

2. Wilma F. Smith and Richard L. Andrews, *Instructional Leadership: How Principals Make a Difference* (Alexandria, Virginia: Association for Supervision and Curriculum Development (1989), 29.

3. Barbara Guzzetti and Michael Martin, "A Comparative Analysis of Elementary and Secondary Principals' Instructional Leadership Behavior," (January 1984): ED245 399.

4. VanCleve Morris et. al.,"The Urban Principal: Middle Manager in the Educational Bureaucracy," *Phi Delta Kappan* (June 1982).

5. Jon Saphier and Robert Gower, *The Skillful Teacher: Building Your Teaching Skills* (Carlisle, Massachusetts: Research for Better Teaching, 1987).

6. Thomas D. Bird and Judith Warren Little, *Instructional Leadership in Eight Secondary Schools. Final Report* (Boulder, Colorado: Center for Action Research, Inc., June, 1985).

CHAPTER SEVEN

STEP SIX Develop Teacher Leaders

What is a teacher leader?

My own personal definition of a teacher leader is an individual who exhibits leadership skills in one or more of the following areas: (1) mentoring and coaching new teachers; (2) collaborating with all staff members, regardless of personal affiliation or preference; (3) learning and growing with a view to bringing new ideas to the classroom and school; (4) polishing writing and presentation skills to share knowledge with others; (5) engaging in creative problem solving and decision making with increased student learning as the goal; (6) being willing to take risks in front of peers; and (7) being willing to share information, ideas, opinions, and evaluative judgments confidently with the instructional leader.

What role do teacher leaders serve?

Effective instructional leaders recognize the importance of sharing responsibility for developing the vision, making decisions, and implementing programs. In her study of excellent high schools, Sara Lawrence Lightfoot highlights this importance:

> *In these good schools the image is one of teachers with voice and vision. Teachers are knowledgeable and discerning school actors who are the primary shapers of the educational environment. They are given a great deal of autonomy and authority in defining the intellectual agenda, but their individual quests are balanced against the requirement that they contribute to the broader school community. Most important, good schools are places that recognize the relationship between the learning and achievement of students and the development and expression of teachers.[1]*

Effective instructional leaders work diligently at helping their teachers develop and express themselves through collaborative and collegial relationships. They value and promote teachers working in teams and willingly give responsibility for decision making to these teams. Judith Warren Little has shown that benefits will return both to the school and the leader from this encouragement:

- Teachers will support one another's strengths and accommodate one another's weaknesses, thereby increasing the total effectiveness of teaching and learning.

- Teachers will be more willing to test new ideas, methods, and materials.

- The instructional program and school culture will be transmitted to new staff members through the explicit training and socializing that take place.[2]

Many instructional leaders have learned the hard way that failure to develop strong teacher leaders and share the yoke of leadership will result in the development of one or more of these four flaws: (1) You won't be open to learning and growing as a person and professional, (2) the quality of learning will be affected, (3) you'll win the battle but lose the war, or (4) you'll burn out "doing it all yourself."

Fullan and Hargreaves have summarized these flaws eloquently:

"My vision," "my teachers," "my school" are proprietary claims and attitudes which suggest an ownership of the school that is personal rather than collective, imposed rather than earned, and hierarchical rather than democratic. With visions as singular as this, teachers soon learn to suppress their voice. It does not get articulated. Management becomes manipulation.[3]

Growing and learning as a professional. Do not make the mistake of thinking you have all the answers and are the fount of all wisdom. This will isolate you from any kind of personal or professional growth. Your staff will learn, in a dangerously fast fashion, that questioning the principal's judgment, sharing a radical idea, or pointing out that "the emperor is indeed stark naked" can all be suicidal acts. They will retreat to their classrooms and the teacher's lounge to grumble to each other. You will miss the opportunity, painful as it may often be, to learn from others.

Improving the quality of student learning. Your focus as an instructional leader should always be student learning. The most powerful force for improving student learning is the collective energy, wisdom, and will of all the teachers in the school learning community. Teachers who see the principal as facilitator, supporter, and reinforcer for the jointly determined school mission rather than a guider, director, and leader of his or her own personal agenda are far more likely to feel personally accountable for student learning. Thomas Sergiovanni points out that in the school communities of the future "leadership will become less and less important, self-management will begin to take hold, and substitutes for leadership will become more deeply embedded in the school."[4]

> "The principal of a successful school is not the instructional leader but the coordinator of teachers as instructional leaders."
>
> Carl Glickman

Giving up a battle to win the war. A classic mistake that many leaders make is to lead the foot soldiers to a successful implementation in some minor skirmish while remaining totally oblivious to the havoc they have created with regard to troop morale or long-term deployment of resources. Many well-meaning instructional leaders have gone down in defeat, usually well documented historically and recounted for centuries, for lack of consulting, working with, and engaging all of the junior officers.

Avoiding burnout. There is a very real danger of growing disillusioned, disheartened, and discouraged if you don't have a group of energized, professional staff surrounding you. The effective instructional leader recognizes that burnout is the all-too-common result of attempting to do everything on his or her own. The sense of isolation, frustration, and anger that often results from being the only cheerleader, resource provider, or "idea" person can demoralize even the most competent of leaders.

What are some ways to develop leaders?

There are five primary ways that teachers can function as leaders in your school:

- Teachers can train and provide staff development for other teachers.
- Teachers can coach and mentor other teachers.
- Teachers can develop and write curriculum.
- Teachers can serve as decision makers and leaders of school teams.
- Teachers can serve as members of teams, committees, task forces, or quality circles.

An important prerequisite to the training and development of teacher leaders in any of these areas, however, must be the encouragement and fostering of a collegial atmosphere in your school. Without collegiality, teacher leaders will wither and die. Their efforts will be poorly received, your motivations as an instructional leader will be suspect, and everyone's time will be wasted. John Mahaffy has described the path, sometimes rocky, from isolation to collegiality. He cites several stopping-off points along the way: autocracy, coordination, accommodation, independence, cooperation, and collaboration.

Mahaffy defines autocracy as a place of solitude where teachers work in isolation. "The autocratic teacher has no real colleagues and is a peer only in the sense there are often more such teachers in the school."[5] Coordination, the second point, is closely related to autocracy but goes beyond to include the fact that all teachers usually play by a common set of rules and agree on calendars, schedules, and other procedural matters.

Accommodation is the next phase. Teachers in this phase use the same textbooks and curricula and interact with their peers in a social way. Independence, the next phase, is seen by Mahaffy as "participatory interdependence." Teachers in this kind of school understand they are part of the larger school and its mission. They work alone but appreciate how what they do connects to others. Cooperation, the next phase, is characterized by teachers getting together to work for the accomplishment of a specific goal. Although they live independently most of the time, when necessary they can and do cooperate to accomplish a task. Collaboration, however, is the ultimate goal for any instructional leader. "In collaboration, people work together and talk to each other about things that matter. People in collaborative schools watch, help, teach, and learn from each other. The major difference between collaboration and other states is that in collaboration teachers and administrators share a common paradigm—a philosophy that guides their decisions and their professionalism."[6]

> **IN-HOUSE STAFF DEVELOPMENT**
>
> Paul Casciano of New York surveys his staff at the end of each school year to gather topics they would like to learn more about. The nine topics of greatest interest are assigned to different members of the faculty, each of whom makes a one-and-one-half-hour presentation. This program keeps everyone growing and learning. About thirty teachers attend the voluntary sessions.

Teachers as trainers. The belief that consultants and experts always do a more effective job as trainers and staff developers can stand in the way of developing teacher leaders. Give your teachers the same kind of professional courtesies and respect you pay a visiting consultant. Pay them for their preparation time. Require that participants sign up in advance for the privilege of hearing them speak. Provide appropriate facilities and equipment to make the presentation more professional. And give your teachers helpful feedback and evaluation so they will continue to improve. Each time a teacher prepares a workshop or presentation for another group of teachers, his or her own teaching performance and effectiveness improves. In my opinion, staff development dollars spent on teachers training teachers will double your investment.

> *Convincing the powers that be that teachers are professionals who learn best from one another is the central issue. In the financial crunch facing so many school districts it would seem easier to "sell" a program that does not require high-priced consultants, expensive materials, and disruption of classes than the more typical inservice experience that often requires all three. Strange as it seems, districts will often pay the price for the legitimacy of the expensive "expert" rather than put those resources into using their own staffs as experts.[7]*

Teachers as curriculum writers/authors. Don't make the mistake of thinking that your teachers can't develop curriculum that will measure up to the highest standards. Send them to workshops, give them time to study and plan together, and when necessary bring in consultants to advise. Then, just let them create. The process won't be perfect in the beginning, but the process is infinitely more important than the product. And the products will begin to improve with practice. Jack Van Leirsburg, principal at Briar Glen School in Glen Ellyn, Illinois, has provided the kind of collaborative atmosphere in his school that has spawned several published authors, among them his learning center teacher, Pat Riggs, and his gifted specialist, Judy Leimbach.

"In an information-rich environment, no single individual is likely to have all the pieces of the puzzle needed to make sense of the situation."

Edward Pajak

Teachers as decision makers (school decision-making teams). If you haven't discovered the power of sharing the leadership of your school with a team of teachers, you've missed one of the most powerful, growth-evoking experiences available to a building principal. Rather than weakening your power base or making you less effective as an instructional leader, sharing leadership will increase your influence. Charles Garfield points out in his study of peak performers that leaders who develop, reward, and recognize those around them are "simply allowing the human assets with which they work to appreciate in value."[8] The schools in West Chicago, Illinois, have employed site-based management and building leadership teams in their six schools since 1985. A team of four teachers—each serving a two-year term—meets monthly for one-half day of release time to solve problems, set goals, design programs, and focus on student learning. The unique populations and challenges of each school result in different agendas for each team, but the focus must always relate to the overall district goal of learning for all.

> **FACULTY MEETINGS
> A LA CARTE**
>
> Gary McDonald's staff members rotate their meetings from classroom to classroom. The staff member hosting the meeting is responsible for a brief explanation of his or her program as well as providing refreshments.

Gene Maeroff has summarized some of the advantages that using the team approach to change can have:

- Teams can set priorities so that too much change is not dumped on the school with no sense of what is most important.

- Teams can model the kinds of behavior that they would like to elicit from colleagues.

- Teams can try to anticipate objections so that the answers are provided before some of the negative reactions are registered.[9]

Teachers as members of committees/task forces/teams. Phyllis O'Connell develops teacher leaders when she asks for volunteers to study new issues (outcomes-based education), become specialists in new curricular areas (hands-on math), or train staff in new techniques (alternative/authentic assessment). These small groups meet on their own with a chairperson and report back to the faculty or building leadership team as necessary. When Phyllis senses that the school should be moving in a new direction, she lets her faculty learn about it on their own. Teachers, rather than the principal, become the chief spokespersons for change. Teams can also be formed as part of the instructional delivery system (grade-level/departmental/interdisciplinary). Or they can be formed on an ad hoc basis to solve disciplinary problems, develop new recognition programs, or assist in selecting new staff members. This approach is widely used in the business world. As Rosabeth Moss Kanter pointed out, "Whether called task forces, quality circles, problem-solving groups, or shared responsibility teams, such vehicles for greater participation are an important part of an innovating company."[10] They are also a necessity for the innovating school and the effective instructional leader.

> **FACULTY LIAISON COUNCIL**
>
> Henry Scipione of Middlebury, Vermont, has organized the faculty into cross-grade teams of seven to eight people per team. Each team chooses one representative to serve on the Liaison Council. The council operates on a one person/one vote concept, including that of the principal, and serves as the decision-making body for the school. Involvement, commitment, accountability, and ownership for decisions increase.

Teachers as researchers. Ann Lieberman and her colleagues believe that involving teachers in "doing research" can develop leadership skills and result in powerful professional development. They suggest three areas for potential interactive research: (1) curricular concerns (How do students learn math concepts best?), (2) instructional concerns (How can time-on-task be increased in my classroom?), and (3) overall professional concerns (What are the factors that contribute to high morale in a school?).[11]

Carol Auer and her teachers at Turner Elementary School in West Chicago, Illinois, are involved in an interactive research study. Working with a team from the Ball Foundation, they are studying the impact of increased parent-teacher interaction in informal settings on student achievement. The teachers involved in the study have gained confidence and leadership skills in many areas as a result of the research: (1) interpersonal communication skills, (2) ability to interact confidently with professionals from other disciplines, (3) ability to talk knowledgeably with other faculty about the home-school connection, and (4) a new understanding of the impact they personally have on students' lives.

How can you keep your team focused?

This is critically important. Anyone who has participated in a leadership team will concur with the observation made by a teacher team member that "you get bogged down in micromanagement: the bathrooms are dirty, the lights are out somewhere, the intercom doesn't work."[12] The focus of the team should be student learning/achievement. Keeping that focus is the key role of the instructional leader. You can do it by setting up guidelines about the types of issues that your team will discuss, the length of time

> **STAFF MEETINGS TOO GOOD TO MISS**
>
> Merry Wade begins every staff meeting with a drawing for a door prize. This gets everyone there on time, and it's fun to be a winner. She brings back t-shirts from conferences and conventions to use as prizes.

you'll devote to noninstructional issues, and by skillful redirection of team members who veer off task.

How can you use group decision making?

Trust and mutual respect are the key elements to successful group decision making and consensus building. The effective instructional leaders use a variety of techniques, for even when a finely tuned school leadership team comes up with an outstanding recommendation, that group still needs to gain the approval and support of the faculty at large.

Dave Burton avoids building consensus on important issues in a large group setting such as a faculty meeting. Instead, he works through his leadership team members or through the team leaders in his middle school. They are individuals in whom he has a great deal of confidence, and he trusts them to communicate effectively with the people they represent. When he feels he has an especially "touchy" issue on the agenda, he finds that pizza and soft drinks have a soothing effect on his staff.

Other instructional leaders hold many informal discussions. Linda Hanson works constantly, organizing small and large group forums to present her ideas and get them talked about. She hastens to add, "Everything is done through mutual respect." Chris Gaylord keeps bringing up agenda items until her faculty has really worked through them. She doesn't rush and waits until teachers have ownership in both the problem and the solutions. Nick Friend goes out and sells his ideas at times. He calls it "gentle, relentless pressure." Some instructional leaders still have difficulty with this skill, particularly if they believe strongly about issues and think that students are suffering. They are impatient for things to happen. They feel frustration at the shortsightedness of some faculty members. "Consensus does not happen as quickly as I would like. I feel that we will never agree on some issues of education. This is hard!" But Alan Jones, principal of West Chicago Community High School, is one who is learning to take the necessary steps:

> *I'm in the process of making a cognitive shift in this area. In order to reach consensus, you must be willing to share information and responsibility. In addition, you should possess communication skills which allow a group to get to a "third alternative."*

The culture of the school must reflect a belief that everyone's ideas are important and will be considered. Effective instructional leaders are never reluctant to "back off" if the entire staff, or a good portion of it, is not willing to move forward on a particular plan or idea; they recognize the importance of listening to the professional staff. The idea may be a good one that needs more time to jell. The idea may be a bad one that has been "sold" by a terrific sales presentation. Or the faculty may have too many other priorities at any time. There are many valid reasons for tabling an issue.

Angie Garcia has summarized a list of particularly helpful guidelines for reaching consensus. But don't assume that everyone will automatically understand and subscribe to these guidelines. Effective instructional leaders spend time training and working with teacher leaders to develop common understandings as well as skills to implement these principles:[13]

- Avoid arguing for your own individual judgments. Present your positions as clearly as possible, but listen to other members' reactions and consider the logic before pressing your point.

- Do not assume that someone must win and someone must lose when discussion reaches a stalemate. Instead, look for the next most acceptable alternative for all. Keep the discussion focused on what you can agree on, even if it is only one small point.

- Do not change your mind simply to avoid conflict. Be suspicious when agreement comes too quickly and easily.

- Avoid conflict-reducing techniques such as majority vote, averaging coin flips, and bargaining. When a dissenting member finally agrees, don't feel that he or she must be rewarded later.

- Differences of opinion are natural and expected. Disagreements can help the group decision because with a wide range of information there is a greater chance that the group will hit upon more adequate solutions.

- When you can't seem to get anywhere in a large group, break into smaller groups and try to reach consensus. Then return to the larger group and try again.

- When one or two members simply can't agree with the group after a reasonable period of time, ask them to deliver a minority report based on their logic.

Judith Dawson has identified three important factors that are necessary if you want to build consensus successfully among staff members:[14]

1. **Give people time.** Teachers need time if you really want to foster a supportive environment that develops teacher leaders and encourages collaborative planning. They need time in other locations—restaurants, conference centers, people's homes; they need time to work with people from other grade levels and disciplines as well as from the same grade levels and disciplines; they need time to solve specific problems; they need time to plan for the future; they need planning meetings at the beginning of the school year; and they need evaluative meetings at the end of the school year.

2. **Spend the time on issues that are really important to your staff.** Never waste teachers' time on issues that are not their responsibility. You will lose credibility, and more important, you will waste valuable time. Teacher time should not be taken up with issues such as lights for the parking lot or which fundraiser to use; those issues can be handled by security and administration, respectively. Their time should be devoted to issues of teaching and learning.

3. **Support the changes that teachers recommend over the long haul.** In the words of one veteran teacher, "Don't ask for my opinion if you aren't prepared to live with the consequences." If you're not prepared to support the changes that teachers recommend, then don't even begin to encourage participatory decision making or develop teacher leaders on your faculty.

How can you maximize your time?

The phrase "quality time" is often used to describe the time that parents and children should spend together. This same phrase can be used to describe the kind of time you and your staff spend together. You can maximize that time by planning and conducting good meetings—faculty meetings, planning meetings, team meetings, grade-level meetings, problem-solving meetings. You will need the ability to lead and follow, listen and summarize, brainstorm, organize, manage conflict, and know when to adjourn.

The instructional leaders we interviewed had these helpful suggestions for planning and organizing effective meetings:

- Provide printed agendas at least two days in advance, if possible.

- Test the water for input ahead of time.

- Be ready to laugh together before working together.

- Appoint someone different at each meeting to chart graphically the proceedings of the meeting so that everyone can see what is being recorded. Use lots of different-colored markers, illustrations, flow charts, and so forth, to make the meeting "come alive" on paper. This will help you summarize the meeting later in a written form. Make sure any decisions reached at the meeting are disseminated as quickly as possible in the days that follow the meeting.

- Expect and reinforce professional behavior. Don't talk when others are talking. Respect other people's ideas and opinions. Be positive.

- Organize in small discussion groups and then culminate with a full faculty meeting.

- Set a beginning and ending time, and never start or end late, even if people are not on time.

- Never make or read announcements to staff members that they can read themselves.

- The principal should be the organizer, not the orator.

- Serve food when appropriate.

- Get everyone involved. Don't allow one or two individuals to monopolize the meeting.

- Give staff members a writing activity at the end of the meeting to focus their thinking and planning.

- If consensus isn't occurring, postpone the decision. Few decisions *must* be made today.

- Make certain that the discussion is moving forward and not in circles.
- Share accomplishments.
- Always end on a positive note.
- Praise, praise, praise!

How can you use the Instructional Leadership Behavioral Checklist to assess your progress toward Step Six: Develop teacher leaders?

There are three indicators that describe Step Six in more detail:

1.	Schedules, plans, or facilitates regular meetings of all types (planning, problem solving, decision making, or inservice/training) among teachers to address instructional issues
2.	Provides opportunities for and training in collaboration, shared decision making, coaching, mentoring, curriculum development, and making presentations
3.	Provides motivation and resources for faculty members to engage in professional growth activities

Every indicator is followed by three sections:

1.	A **comment** that defines the specifications of the indicator
2.	A **scale of descriptors** that gives a continuum of behaviors (1-5) from least effective to most effective
3.	**Key points in the descriptors** that give detailed explanations of each of the five items in the scale

For each indicator, select the number from 1 to 5 that most accurately describes your own behavior on a day-to-day basis.

INSTRUCTIONAL LEADERSHIP
BEHAVIORAL CHECKLIST

STEP SIX: Develop teacher leaders.

Indicator 6.1 Schedules, plans, or facilitates regular meetings of all types (planning, problem solving, decision making, or inservice/training) among teachers to address instructional issues

Comment:

The main focus of Indicator 6.1 is both the quantity and quality of meetings that discuss instructional issues.

SCALE OF DESCRIPTORS:

1. Few meetings are held, instructional issues are never discussed, and no shared decision making or collaboration occurs.

2. Meetings are held on an "as needed" basis, instructional issues are rarely discussed, and no shared decision making or collaboration occurs.

3. Meetings are regularly scheduled, instructional issues are sometimes discussed, and some shared decision making and collaboration occur.

4. Meetings are regularly scheduled, instructional issues are discussed on an "as needed" basis, and some shared decision making and collaboration are evident.

5. Meetings of all types are regularly scheduled, instructional issues are discussed on a continuing basis, and shared decision making and collaboration characterize all meetings.

KEY POINTS IN DESCRIPTORS

1. Few meetings held, no instructional discussions, no shared decision making or collaboration

2. Few meetings held, rare instructional discussions, no shared decision making or collaboration

3. Regularly scheduled meetings, some instructional discussions, some shared decision making and collaboration

4. Regularly scheduled meetings, regularly scheduled instructional discussions, some shared decision making and collaboration

5. Regularly scheduled meetings with continuing discussion of instructional issues, collaboration and shared decision making

Indicator 6.2 Provides opportunities for and training in collaboration, shared decision making, coaching, mentoring, curriculum development, and making presentations

Comment:

The main focus of Indicator 6.2 is the provision of opportunities as well as provision of training in all areas of teacher leadership.

SCALE OF DESCRIPTORS:

1. Principal never provides opportunities or training for teachers to develop leadership skills.

2. Principal provides some opportunities and training for teachers to develop leadership skills but does so in a highly controlled and regulated fashion.

3. Principal provides some opportunities and training for teachers to develop leadership skills but permits a great deal of latitude in the exercise of these skills and does not utilize them or focus them in an organized way.

4. Principal provides a multitude of opportunities and training for teachers to develop leadership skills and utilizes these skills to improve instruction, coordinate with building mission, and improve student learning.

5. Principal provides a multitude of opportunities and training for teachers to develop leadership skills, utilizes them to continually improve instruction in classrooms, and has a school leadership team that participates in the continual improvement of the school.

KEY POINTS IN DESCRIPTORS:

1. No opportunities or training

2. Some opportunities and training but not relevant to needs

3. Opportunities and training provided that are relevant to faculty needs

4. Opportunities and training provided that are relevant to faculty needs and relate to improvement of instruction

5. Opportunities and training provided that are relevant to faculty needs; relate to improvement of instruction; are jointly planned, evaluated, and followed up; and include a systematic school improvement process under the leadership of a school team

Indicator 6.3 Provides motivation and resources for faculty members to engage in professional growth activities

Comment:

The focus of Indicator 6.3 is the encouragement provided by the principal to faculty members either by personal example or positive reinforcement, as well as the allocation of available resources to support proessional growth activities.

SCALE OF DESCRIPTORS:

1. Principal never engages in personal professional growth activities and discourages teachers from doing so by failing to allocate resources for this activity in the budget.

2. Principal never engages in personal professional growth activities and, although monies are available for teacher activities, does not motivate or positively reinforce those teachers who take advantage of them.

3. Principal engages in personal professional growth activities and allocates resources for teachers to do so as well but does not motivate or positively reinforce those teachers who do so.

4. Principal engages in personal professional growth activities, allocates resources for teachers to do so as well, and motivates and positively reinforces those teachers who do so.

5. Principal engages in personal professional growth activities, allocates available resources for teachers to do so as well, motivates teachers to engage in activities that will benefit the building's instructional program, and utilizes their expertise in sharing with other teachers.

KEY POINTS IN DESCRIPTORS:

1. No personal growth activities, no motivation or reinforcement, no resources for teachers

2. No personal growth activities, no motivation or reinforcement, some allocation of resources

3. Personal growth activities, allocation of resources, no motivation or reinforcement

4. Personal growth activities, allocation of available resources, motivation and reinforcement

5. Personal growth activities, allocation of resources, motivation and reinforcement, utilization of teachers in building activities

117

Notes

1. Sara Lawrence Lightfoot, from a paper presented as the Maycie K. Southall Distinguished Lecture on Public Education and the Futures of Children, Vanderbilt University, Nashville, Tennessee (October 1985): 24.

2. Judith Warren Little, "Teachers as Colleagues," in *Educators' Handbook: A Research Perspective,* D. Berliner et. al., eds. (New York: Longman, 1987), 491-518.

3. Michael G. Fullan and A. Hargreaves, *What's Worth Fighting For? Working Together for Your School* (Toronto: Ontario Public School Teachers' Federation, 1991), 90.

4. Thomas J. Sergiovanni, "Why We Should Seek Substitutes for Leadership," *Educational Leadership* (February 1992): 42.

5. John E. Mahaffy, *Collegial Support System: A Process Model Draft* (Portland, Oregon: Northwest Regional Educational Laboratory, (1988), 12-15.

6. Ibid.

7. S. S. Roper and D. E. Hoffman, "Collegial Support for Professional Improvement: The Stanford Collegial Evaluation Program" *OSSC* (Oregon School Study Council) *Bulletin,* 29(7) (1986): 24.

8. Charles Garfield, *Peak Performers: The New Heroes of American Business* (New York: William Morrow and Company, Inc., 1986), 182.

9. Gene I. Maeroff, "Building Teams to Rebuild Schools," *Phi Delta Kappan* (March 1993): 515.

10. Rosabeth Moss Kanter, *The Change Masters: Innovation and Entrepreneurship in the American Corporation* (New York: Simon & Schuster, 1983), 241.

11. Ann Lieberman, "Collaborative Research: Working With, Not Working On" *Educational Leadership* (February 1986): 28-32.

12. Ann Bradley and Lynn Olson, "The Balance of Power," *Education Week* (February 24, 1993): 11.

13. Angie Garcia, "Consensus Decision-Making Promotes Involvement, Ownership, Satisfaction." *NASSP Bulletin* (November 1986): 50-2.

14. Judith Dawson, *The Principal's Role in Facilitating Teacher Participation: Mediating the Influence of School Context* (Washington, D.C.: National Institute of Education, 1984), 15.

CHAPTER EIGHT

Step Seven
Maintain Positive Attitudes Toward Students, Staff, and Parents

HOW SHOULD YOU SERVE AS AN ADVOCATE FOR STUDENTS?

WHAT ARE THE KEY HUMAN RELATIONS SKILLS?

WHAT DOES RESEARCH SAY?

HOW CAN YOU DEVELOP MORALE?

HOW CAN YOU ACKNOWLEDGE THE ACHIEVEMENTS OF OTHERS

HOW CAN YOU USE THE INSTRUCTIONAL LEADERSHIP BEHAVIORAL CHECKLIST?

James Autry, in his book *Love and Profit: The Art of Caring Leadership,* says, "Good management is largely a matter of love. Or if you are uncomfortable with that word, call it caring."[1] The Apostle Paul put it this way. "If I had the gift of being able to speak in tongues, and could speak in every language there is in all of heaven and earth, but I didn't love others, it would be of no value whatever. I would only be making a lot of noise."[2] Stephen Covey calls it seeking first to understand rather than to be understood.[3] Autry, the Apostle Paul, and Covey have all discovered and articulated a principle that effective instructional leaders seek to practice in their daily lives—attitudes and relationships are the key.

The leadership literature is replete with examples of individuals who have the necessary competence to do the job—they just don't have people skills. There are many well-meaning administrators who have all of the necessary certification, know good instruction, and even have a vision of what their school could and should become. But they are remarkably like Ed, a CEO described for us by Warren Bennis:

Fostering and maintaining positive attitudes toward students, staff, and parents is critical to effectiveness as an instructional leader. As two of my colleagues noted,

> *I want to be viewed as a person who listens and cares for each person as an individual. I shake hands with children, bus drivers, moms, dads, grandparents, neighbors, and pet the dogs. I have strong opinions about education and life, but I try to treat all people who enter the building as customers. I enjoy my profession and it shows.*

> *I believe that I can work with just about any type of individual. I don't expect perfection from anyone, but I do expect hard work, a sincere interest in children, and dedication. I have the ability to listen. I listen to angry parents and hurt teachers, but it's very rare that they leave angry or hurt.*

How should you serve as an advocate for students?

The instructional leaders we interviewed see student advocacy as a part of their overall vision and mission. "The whole point of everything we do is for students," said Linda Hanson. Frances Starks adds, "Students are the reason we have our jobs, and we owe them the best of what we have to give. Their concern and development come first."

Effective instructional leaders don't just talk about how much they care about students. They do things. On a daily basis, they work to change policies and practices in the areas of discipline, grading, and grouping; they volunteer in a variety of community activities; they develop close personal relationships with students; and their doors are always open.

Discipline. While effective instructional leaders believe in the importance of discipline and are firm and fair disciplinarians, they also recognize that the system doesn't always work for students. Carol Auer often pleads that students be given the benefit of the doubt and frequently enlightens teachers about a situation that may change their views of a child's behavior. Alan Jones is similarly motivated:

> *I investigate all student complaints about teachers or implementation of policies. I will intervene aggressively if I feel a student has been wronged. You really walk a tightrope in this area. Teachers are sensitive to the support issue. But I think you must send a message that students are people and deserve an audience.*

Grading practices. Effective instructional leaders also intervene as student advocates when grading practices seem unfair. "All of us have tunnel vision about our jobs," Brent McArdle believes. "Bringing a student perspective to something like grading practices sometimes keeps a teacher from being too myopic."

Community. Student advocacy is not limited to the hours that school is in session. For some instructional leaders a commitment to students extends nearly twenty-four hours a day. Mike Pettibone is involved in Little League, Saturday intramurals, Saturday enrichments, and Friday Night Prime Times, and even serves as a reading buddy at the public library.

Instructional issues. It is in the area of student learning that instructional leaders are eloquent advocates for students. "I

"We discovered [in good high schools] that the qualities traditionally identified as female—nurturance, receptivity, responsiveness to relationships and context—are critical to the expression of a noncaricatured masculine leadership. Good leaders redefine the classic male domain of high school principals. In good high schools students are treated with fearless and empathetic attention by adults."

Sara Lawrence Lightfoot

am constantly striving for quality instructional time, attention to individual differences, and programs that allow the active participation of all children regardless of ability," says Richard Seyler. Bob Hassan knows each and every student—his or her strengths, weaknesses, and needs. He is intimately involved in all program reviews, placement decisions, and academic conferences.

Counselor, listener, and friend. Effective instructional leaders care about students. Nick and Maryanne Friend both have wonderful personal relationships with their students. Their students are keenly aware that the Friends are really "true friends." They attend activities, show affection, and acknowledge successes. They take students to lunch and send personal cards and notes. Students are also willing to confide in Dave Burton, because, "based on the number of students who come to me with problems or just to talk, I feel that they trust me. They know that my primary purpose is to work with them, and they know that my door is always open to them."

What are the key human relations skills?

Effective instructional leaders are confident about their human relations skills. They are able to articulate what they do well and are always willing to learn. Nancy Carbone summarized it this way:

> *I think the main human relations skill I possess is the willingness to give people a voice in the daily business of the school. I firmly believe that inviting people to participate in decision making is what makes a school work best. I am also willing to admit when I am wrong and to change a course of action if most of the staff feel it is not advisable for the school.*

Instructional leaders are unanimous in selecting the one skill they believe is essential—listening. And they highlight the following aspects of effective listening as particularly important:

CONFLICT MANAGERS

Fred Merten, principal of Irving Elementary School in Eugene, Oregon, trains fourth- and fifth-grade students in conflict resolution. These students are available at recess time to assist other students with misunderstandings, arguments, pushing matches, fights, and so on.

- Make eye contact.
- Give your undivided attention.
- Send nonverbal signals that you are interested and that you care; for example, don't shuffle papers or keep on writing.
- Be able to restate or rephrase what is being said when appropriate.
- Don't interrupt. Instructional leaders are constantly being interrupted, but you must guard against sending the message to teachers that you don't have time to talk.

In addition to the skill of listening, there are countless other human relations skills that are also important. The following were cited by many of the instructional leaders we interviewed:

- Be willing to admit when you're wrong.
- Be able to laugh and cry.
- Take time to help others.
- Remember how it felt to be a child.
- Be able to resolve conflicts among people.
- Remain calm in stressful situations.
- Be able to work with people of all ages.
- Truly care about others.
- Realize that you can't please everyone.
- Be optimistic about people's motives.

> "While large meetings and grand symbolic actions play a part, the most significant change in work culture is accomplished in one-to-one personal interactions."
>
> Richard D. Sagor

What does research say?

There are hundreds of principals who have almost every quality that makes a good instructional leader, yet they have failed miserably in their jobs because they couldn't communicate. They were lacking one or more of the eight basic communication skills identified by Charles Jung and his colleagues: listening, asking questions, paraphrasing, agreeing and disagreeing, describing behavior, describing feelings, checking perceptions, and giving feedback.[5]

Of the eight skills, most of us seem to focus on agreeing and disagreeing and giving feedback. We want to move immediately to solving problems or giving our opinions, when what we should focus on are the other six aspects of communication.

Listening. Good listeners don't interrupt, judge, answer before thinking, or give off negative nonverbal signals. Instead they face the speaker, are aware of biases or values that might distort what they are hearing, and concentrate on what is being said.[6]

Asking questions. Asking questions makes the other person feel as if you are really interested in what is being said. Concentrate on asking questions that are open-ended. If a yes or no answer will suffice, communication is halted. Probe for details, examples, and impressions.

Paraphrasing. This aspect of communication has been stressed so vigorously in the popular literature that some people can become downright tiresome in their attempts to be empathetic. There is a real need, however, for periodic checking for understanding. "Let me see if I have that correctly. Is this what you mean?"

Agreeing and disagreeing. When you agree with others, everyone feels good. You have mutual interests, and you will be able to work together well. Disagreeing takes a bit more finesse. Find some area of commonality before you disagree. But then be prepared to express your difference of opinion. You are obligated as one of the members in the dyad or larger group to state some opinion about the topic under discussion.

Describing behavior. Jung and his colleagues warn against making evaluative statements when describing someone's behavior. They cite several types of supportive communication that can reduce defensiveness:

- Solving the problem rather than controlling the situation
- Being spontaneous rather than following a strategy
- Empathizing rather than remaining neutral
- Relating to others as equals, rather than superiors or subordinates
- Approaching differences of opinion with openness to new perspectives rather than dogmatism

Describing feelings. It is important to be up front about your feelings. No one appreciates dissembling. But neither are most of us ready for bluntness or crudeness. Concentrate on being precise in describing how you feel, using the pronouns "I," "me," and "my."

Checking Perceptions. This is different from but related to paraphrasing. It simply means that you are trying to determine whether your impressions of another person's feelings are accurate.

Giving feedback. Good instructional leaders are as ready to give feedback (especially positive) as they are to receive feedback (especially negative) about themselves. Effective instructional leaders constantly give positive feedback to staff, students, and parents.

FIRESIDE CHATS

Nicholas Gledich at the Windermere Elementary School in Windermere, Florida, has a unique way of communicating with students. Ten to twelve times a year he makes a home video from his living room, sitting in his favorite chair near the fireplace. These short presentations feature a variety of topics including current events, behavior/manners, favorite books, or drug awareness discussions. He then shows the videos on closed-circuit television.

How can you develop morale?

Morale as defined by Webster is "a mental condition with respect to several characteristics," among them confidence and enthusiasm. Morale in a school setting is an integral part of the culture of the school—the feelings you get when you walk in the building, how people treat each other, how they feel about their work, and how they talk about what they do. When morale is poor, people have a sense of powerlessness. Teachers feel powerless to affect students, and students feel like pawns and puppets whose only recourse is to revolt.

Parents also feel manipulated and used. Many effective instructional leaders have been hired into just such a setting.

How have they built morale? They have accomplished it by using simple methods, such as sending out questionnaires and then listening carefully to people's responses. Linda Murphy of Hinsdale, Illinois, has served as principal in several schools and districts. Because she is an avid learner and practitioner of the school culture literature, her first act on assuming the principalship is always to ask the following important questions of all staff. She may do this in a written questionnaire, small focus or discussion groups, or individual conferences.

- As your new building principal, how can I best support you this school year?
- What are XYZ School's most recent successes?
- How do you think XYZ School ought to change?
- What is one thing that you are most excited about this year?
- What do you like most and least about working at XYZ School? ABC District?
- What causes you the greatest stress in your work?
- What is important to the parents of XYZ School?
- What are our students like?
- What format for decision making would you recommend at the building level?
- What curriculum issues need attention at XYZ School?
- What are your overall impressions of XYZ School— its strengths and weaknesses?
- What is the key issue that XYZ School faces in the near future? What should I know about this issue? How should it be resolved?
- How are important decisions made relative to XYZ School? How effective is this process? Should it be changed? If so, how?

- What are you proudest of, relative to ABC District/
  XYZ School? What is your proudest accomplishment
  while working at XYZ School?
- What would you like me to know that I have not asked?

With the information she receives from this questionnaire, Murphy has a clear picture of the morale in her new school. She also has a list of priorities for morale building, if needed, and knows exactly where to begin working with teachers, parents, and students.

How can you acknowledge the achievements of others?

Acknowledging the earned achievements of others is part of morale building, but it must happen in an atmosphere of honesty, collegiality, and caring. There is nothing more devastating to morale than phony praise calculated to accomplish hidden agendas. Praise and celebration must be grounded in the mission of the school, embedded in the culture of the community, and sincerely given in the spirit of appreciation and caring. The recognition of accomplishments must be shared by all and appreciated by all.

Here are some ways that outstanding instructional leaders acknowledge the accomplishments of students, teachers, and parents:

- **Celebrate success.** Kindergarten through sixth-
  grade students are recognized monthly for success in
  one of three areas—Academic, Behavior, or
  Citizenship—at the Allenwood School in Allenwood,
  New Jersey. Students in the second through sixth
  grades at Lincoln Elementary School in West Chicago,
  Illinois, were recognized quarterly for academic
  success by joining the A-Team. They received T-shirts
  the first time they made the team and iron-on stars
  each subsequent time. Local merchants sponsored the
  "team" and underwrote the cost of the shirts.
- **Golden Apple awards.** Ann Parker, elementary

principal in Canton, Missouri, presents Golden Apple awards to staff members and homerooms that have made a noteworthy contribution to improving the school climate. The recipient is presented with a small brass apple that remains with them for the week. It is then passed on to the next Golden Apple winner.

- **Parent Hall of Fame.** In an effort to make the school a welcome place for parents, a prominent area in the lobby of Nancy Carbone's school in Greenwich, Connecticut, has been designated as the Parent Hall of Fame. Each month, individual parents and/or groups of parents are nominated to be honored. The school media specialist photographs the individuals and creates an ongoing attractive display.

- **Get it while it's hot.** Joyce Roberts of Farmington, New Mexico, carries a small tape recorder with her as she walks through the halls to record student work displays. Upon returning to her office she hands the tape to her secretary, who makes certificates to give to staff and/or students who are deserving of special recognition.

- **Congratulations.** At the end of each semester, the president of the local bank in Boaz, Alabama, sends letters of congratulations to honor roll students at Amelia Cartrett's school. The bank has adopted the school, and the letters are just another way of recognizing the achievements of students.

- **Cracker Jack job.** When a faculty or staff member does an exceptional job or gives that extra effort for a project or activity, Danny Shaw at the Calhoun Elementary School in Anderson, South Carolina, acknowledges him or her with a personal thank-you note and a box of Cracker Jacks.

How can you use the Instructional Leadership Behavioral Checklist to assess your progress toward Step Seven: Maintain positive attitudes toward students, staff, and parents?

There are seven indicators that describe Step Seven in more detail:

1.	Serves as an advocate of students and communicates with them regarding aspects of their school life
2.	Encourages open communication among staff members and maintains respect for differences of opinion
3.	Demonstrates concern and openness in the consideration of student, teacher, and/or parent problems and participates in the resolution of such problems where appropriate
4.	Models appropriate human relations skills
5.	Develops and maintains high morale
6.	Systematically collects and responds to staff, student, and parent concerns
7.	Acknowledges appropriately the earned achievements of others

"You're not sure when you engage in synergistic communication how things will work out or what the end will look like, but you do have an inward sense of excitement and security and adventure, believing that it will be significantly better than before."

Stephen R. Covey

Every indicator is followed by three sections:

1.	A **comment** that defines the specifications of the indicator
2.	A **scale of descriptors** that gives a continuum of behaviors (1-5) from least effective to most effective
3.	**Key points in the descriptors** that give detailed explanations of each of the five items in the scale

For each indicator, select the number from 1 to 5 that most accurately describes your own behavior on a day-to-day basis.

INSTRUCTIONAL LEADERSHIP
BEHAVIORAL CHECKLIST

STEP SEVEN: Maintain positive attitudes toward students, staff, and parents.

Indicator 7.1 Serves as an advocate of students and communicates with them regarding aspects of their school life

---

Comment:

The main focus of Indicator 7.1 is on the behaviors the principal exhibits that give evidence of student advocacy and interaction with students. Behaviors might include lunch with individual students or groups; frequent appearances on the playground, in the lunchroom and in hallways; sponsorship of clubs; availability to students who wish to discuss instructional or disciplinary concerns; knowledge of students' names and family relationships; addressing the majority of students by name; and willingness to listen to the student's side in a faculty/student problem. The preceding list is meant ONLY to suggest the types of behaviors that might be appropriate for consideration in this category.

SCALE OF DESCRIPTORS:

1. Principal does not feel that acting as a student advocate is an appropriate role of the principal and never interacts with students.

2. Principal does not feel that acting as a student advocate is an appropriate role of the principal and rarely interacts with students.

3. Principal does not feel that acting as a student advocate is an appropriate role of the principal but engages in at least three behaviors that encourage communication between student and principal.

4. Principal feels that acting as a student advocate is an appropriate role of the principal and engages in at least six behaviors that encourage communication between student and principal.

5. Principal feels that acting as a student advocate is an appropriate role of the principal, engages in at least six behaviors that encourage communication between student and principal, and has established some means of receiving input from students regarding their opinions of school life.

1. No role as an advocate, no interaction with students

2. No role as an advocate, rare interaction with students

3. No role as an advocate, three behaviors that encourage communication

4. Role as an advocate, six behaviors that encourage communication

5. Role as an advocate, six behaviors that encourage communication, some means of receiving student input

Indicator 7.2 Encourages open communication among staff members and maintains respect for differences of opinion

Comment:

The main focus of Indicator 7.2 is on the behaviors the principal exhibits that give evidence of maintenance of open communication among staff members and respect for differences of opinion. Behaviors might include an open-door policy in the principal's office, acceptance of unpopular ideas and negative feedback from faculty, provision of channels for faculty members to voice grievances or discuss problems, and/or provision of channels for faculty members to discuss their work with each other. The preceding list is meant ONLY to suggest the types of behaviors that might be appropriate for consideration in this category.

SCALE OF DESCRIPTORS:

1. Principal does not encourage open communication among staff members and considers differences of opinion to be a sign of disharmony within the organization.

2. Principal supports open communication but is rarely available for informal encounters with staff members. Appointments must be scheduled, meeting agendas are tightly maintained, and the flow of information and opinions is artificially controlled.

3. Principal supports open communication and is available for informal encounters with staff members. Principal is not responsive, however, to problems, questions, or dis-agreements and shuts off communication of this nature.

4. Principal supports open communication and is available for informal encounters with staff members. Principal is responsive to problems, questions, or disagreements, and encourages staff members to work through differences of opinion in positive ways.

5. Principal supports open communication and is available for informal encounters with staff members. An "open-door" policy exists with regard to all problems, questions, and disagreements. Principal structures a variety of opportunities for faculty members to interact both formally and informally, encouraging interaction between grade levels/departments/instructional teams.

KEY POINTS IN DESCRIPTORS:

1. Discourages open communication

2. Exhibits few behaviors that encourage open communication

3. Exhibits some behaviors that encourage open communication

4. Exhibits many behaviors that encourage open communication and facilitates problem solving among staff members

5. Exhibits many behaviors that encourage open communication, facilitates problem solving among staff members, and structures many opportunities for staff interaction

Indicator 7.3 Demonstrates concern and openness in the consideration of student, teacher, and/or parent problems and participates in the resolution of such problems where appropriate

Comment:

The main focus of Indicator 7.3 is the behaviors the principal exhibits in the consideration of problems.

SCALE OF DESCRIPTORS:

1. Principal does not wish to be involved in the consideration of student, teacher, and/or parent problems.

2. Principal is willing to be involved in the consideration of student, teacher, and/or parent problems but is largely ineffective because of poor communication and human relations skills.

3. Principal is willing to be involved in the consideration of student, teacher, and/or parent problems and is sometimes effective in bringing problems to resolution; exhibits average communication and human relations skills.

4. Principal is willing to be involved in the consideration of student, teacher, and/or parent problems and is usually effective in bringing problems to resolution; exhibits excellent communication and human relations skills.

5. Principal is willing to be involved in the consideration of student, teacher, and/or parent problems and is nearly always effective in bringing problems to resolution; exhibits outstanding communication and human relations skills; has

established procedures jointly with faculty for the resolution of problems.

KEY POINTS IN DESCRIPTORS:

1. No involvement

2. Some involvement, ineffective problem solver

3. Involvement, average problem-solving skills

4. Involvement, excellent problem-solving skills

5. Involvement, outstanding problem-solving skills

Indicator 7.4 Models appropriate human relations skills

Comment:

The main focus of Indicator 7.4 is the variety of appropriate human relations skills that are exhibited by the principal. Behaviors MUST include but are not necessarily be limited to establishing a climate of trust and security for students and staff; respecting the rights of students, parents, and staff; handling individual relationships tactfully and with understanding; and accepting the dignity and worth of individuals without regard to appearance, race, creed, sex, ability or disability, or social status.

SCALE OF DESCRIPTORS:

1. Principal has almost no human relations skills.

2. Principal has marginal human relations skills.

3. Principal has average human relations skills.

4. Principal has excellent human relations skills.

5. Principal has outstanding human relations skills.

KEY POINTS IN DESCRIPTORS:

1. Principal exhibits none of the behaviors listed in the Comment section.

2. Principal exhibits only one or two of the behaviors listed in the Comment section and often has difficulty with tasks that involve human interaction.

3. Principal exhibits two or three of the behaviors listed in the Comment section and is usually successful with tasks that involve human interaction.

4. Principal exhibits three or four of the behaviors listed in the Comment section and is frequently successful with tasks that involve human interaction.

5. Principal exhibits all of the behaviors listed in the Comment section as well as many other behaviors associated with good human relations and is almost always successful with tasks that involve human interaction.

Indicator 7.5 Develops and maintains high morale

Comment:

The main focus of Indicator 7.5 is the variety of behaviors exhibited by the principal that contribute to the development and maintenance of high morale. Behaviors might include but not necessarily be limited to involvement of staff in planning, encouragement of planned social events, openness in the dissemination of information, equity in the division of responsibility and allocation of resources, opportunities for achievement, recognition for achievements, involvement of the staff in problem solving, and assistance and support with personal and professional problems.

SCALE OF DESCRIPTORS:

1. Morale is nonexistent in the school building. Principal exhibits none of the behaviors listed in the Comment section. There is little unity among staff members, leading to competition, clique formation, destructive criticism, disagreement, and verbal quarreling.

2. Morale is marginal in the school building. Principal exhibits few of the behaviors listed in the Comment section. Although fewer visible signs of disunity are evident, faculty members nevertheless do not work well together and have negative feelings about their work.

3. Morale is average. Although there are no visible signs of disunity as seen in Descriptor One, teachers work largely as individuals, rarely working together cooperatively with enthusiasm and positive feelings.

4. Morale is excellent. Morale-building behaviors by the principal result in teachers working together to share ideas and resources, identify instructional problems, define mutual goals, and coordinate their activities.

5. Morale is outstanding. Morale-building behaviors by the principal result in teachers working together in a highly effective way while gaining personal satisfaction from their work. Principal has identified specific activities that build morale and systematically engages in these activities.

1. Nonexistent morale

2. Marginal morale

3. Average morale

4. Excellent morale

5. Outstanding morale

Indicator 7.6 Systematically collects and responds to student, staff, and parent concerns

Comment:

The main focus of Indicator 7.6 is the responsiveness of the principal to the regularly solicited and collected concerns of students, staff, and parents. Examples of vehicles used to collect information might include but not necessarily be limited to one-on-one conferences, parent or faculty advisory committees, student council meetings, suggestion boxes, and quality circles.

SCALE OF DESCRIPTORS:

1. No information is collected from students, staff, or parents, and principal is unresponsive to concerns of these groups.

2. Although information is sporadically collected from groups, principal is largely ineffective in responding to concerns.

3. Information is systematically collected from at least one of the three groups, and the principal is effective in responding to concerns.

4. Information is systematically collected from at least two of the three groups, and the principal is effective in responding to concerns.

5. Information is systematically collected from students, staff, and parents; principal is effective in responding to concerns; and information is utilized in planning and implementing change.

KEY POINTS IN DESCRIPTORS:

1. No information, unresponsive principal

2. Sporadic information, ineffective principal

3. Systematic information from one group, effective principal

4. Systematic information from two groups, effective principal

5. Systematic information from three groups, effective principal, utilization of information to plan change

Indicator 7.7 Acknowledges appropriately the earned achievements of others

Comment:

The main focus in Indicator 7.7 is the variety of activities engaged in by the principal that demonstrate the ability to recognize the contributions of students, staff, and parents. Activities might include but are not necessarily limited to staff recognition programs, student award assemblies, certificates, congratulatory notes, phone calls, recognition luncheons, and newspaper articles.

SCALE OF DESCRIPTORS:

1. Principal engages in no recognition activities.

2. Principal engages in at least one recognition activity for one of the three groups.

3. Principal engages in at least one recognition activity for two of the three groups.

4. Principal engages in at least one recognition activity for all three groups.

5. In addition to a variety of recognition activities, the principal involves all three groups in recognition activities for one another.

KEY POINTS IN DESCRIPTORS:

1. No recognition activities

2. One recognition for one of three groups

3. One recognition for two of three groups

4. One recognition for each of the three groups

5. Many recognition activities, with focus on groups recognizing each other

Notes

1. James Autry, *Love and Profit: The Art of Caring Leadership* (New York: William Morrow and Company, Inc., 1991), 13.

2. I Corinthians 13:1, *The Living Bible* (Wheaton, Illinois: Tyndale House Publishers, Inc., 1971), 1160.

3. Stephen R. Covey, *The Seven Habits of Highly Effective People: Restoring the Character Ethic* (New York: Simon & Schuster, 1989).

4. Warren Bennis, *On Becoming a Leader* (Reading, Massachusetts: Addison-Wesley Publishing Company, Inc., 1989), 29.

5. Charles Jung et. al., *Interpersonal Communications: Participant Materials and Leader's Manual* (Portland, Oregon: Northwest Regional Educational Laboratory, 1973), 27.

6. Richard Gemmet, *A Monograph on Interpersonal Communications* (Redwood City, California: San Mateo County Superintendent of Schools, 1977), 33.

CHAPTER NINE

Putting It All Together: Becoming an Instructional Leader

WHAT ARE THE SEVEN ESSENTIAL STEPS TO BECOMING AN EFFECTIVE INSTRUCTIONAL LEADER?

WHAT CAN YOU DO TO GET STARTED?

What are the seven essential steps to becoming an effective instructional leader?

In Chapter One, I suggested several barriers to becoming an instructional leader—lack of skills and training; lack of support from superintendents, school boards, and community; or lack of vision, will, and courage. But I also suggested that anyone with desire could overcome these barriers. Implementing the seven steps to effective instructional leadership is not something you are going to "do" to your school or teachers, but something you are going to "do" to yourself. Let's briefly review the seven steps and then look at what you might do to begin.

Establish and implement instructional goals. This is what Stephen Covey calls beginning with the end in mind. Knowing what you want your graduates to be able to know,

137

do, and be is critical for effectiveness as an instructional leader. *The focus of Step One is on knowing where you're going—the destination of your journey.* Where will the wagons be heading when they pull out of the last outpost?

Be there for your staff. This step has less to do with offering support to someone if they're feeling blue or need a shoulder to cry on than with being an instructional resource and providing the kind of encouragement and motivation teachers need to improve the instructional program. *The focus of Step Two is making sure that the people with whom you're traveling know where they can go for help whenever they need it.* When the wagon breaks down or the provisions run short, you'll be there to shoot a wild turkey or replace a broken wagon wheel.

Create a school culture and climate conducive to learning. Your assignment in Step Three is to make sure that everything that happens in your school is focused on one goal—learning. Time is being used effectively, programs and activities encourage learning, and all teachers and students believe that all can learn. *The focus of Step Three is making sure that nothing interferes with reaching your destination.* You'll head off stampedes of wild buffalo, help the wagons cross the raging rapids, and make sure that everyone is still heading west.

Communicate the vision and mission of your school. Everyone loses his or her way at times. We become distracted by failure, competing agendas, personal problems, or less-meaningful goals. Step Four simply means that you will continually find ways to reassert, rephrase, refocus, and revitalize your mission. *The focus of Step Four is making sure that nobody forgets your goal (the destination of your journey).* You'll circulate through the camp each night to talk about the glories of unexplored lands and the excitement of walking through uncharted territories and to retell the story of the triumphs over tragedy that have already occurred on the trip.

"You can and should shape your own future, because if you don't someone else surely will."

Joel Barker

"Intimacy rises from translating personal and corporate values into daily work practices, from searching for knowledge and wisdom and justice. Above all, intimacy is one way of describing the relationship we all desire with work."

Max DePree

Set high expectations for your staff. Teachers serve at the critical point of instructional delivery. They need to be peak performers every minute of every day. You will help them become those peak performers through observation, feedback, mentoring, and coaching. *The focus of Step Five is making sure that all the pioneers have the tools and talents to go with you on the journey.* You'll encourage every member of the caravan to do his or her very best, offering words of encouragement and assistance whenever needed.

Develop teacher leaders. Teachers have a dual role to play in reaching the goal of learning for all students. Not only will they manage instruction, but they will share in the decision making and leading. *The focus of Step Six is making sure that everyone shares the leadership and responsibility for reaching the destination.* When you grow weary, you'll ask others to act as wagon master.

Maintain positive attitudes toward students, staff, and parents. While you, the instructional leader, are doing all of these other important things (setting goals, communicating the mission, setting high expectations, and bringing out the leader in everyone), remember to keep focused on what's important—people. *The focus of Step Seven is making sure that after you've reached the goal (destination), everybody still likes each other when they get there.* The journey will be characterized by good times around the campfire and satisfaction at pulling through the mudholes as a team.

What can you do to get started?

Don't put off until tomorrow what really needs to begin today. Think now about what you can do to change your instructional leadership behaviors. Here are some of the things effective, experienced instructional leaders do regularly:

Use self-assessment. Spend a few moments, now that

"Thinking is the most important act of leadership in a change-oriented environment."

Phillip Schlechty

"Futurists have a tantalizing way of describing the year 2001 as though being there has little to do with getting there. The future simply arrives full-blown. But it is the succession of days and years between now and then that will determine what life will be like. Decisions made and not made will shape the schools of tomorrow."

John Goodlad

you have completed this book, to administer the McEwan Instructional Leadership Behavioral Checklist to yourself. Be honest in your answers and use the information to help you set personal and professional goals. The complete instrument along with a response form can be found in the Appendix.

Use informal assessment procedures with your staff. Don't wait for others to tell you where you need to improve. Ask them. When I first began this process it was painful. I divided my faculty into four groups—one for each of my building leadership team members. They summarized the answers to each of these questions: "What am I doing that is effective and should be continued?" "What am I doing that is ineffective and should be stopped?" "What am I not doing that I should be doing?" I met with each team member individually, and they shared with me what the teachers had said. There were moments of pain and disbelief. Surely I couldn't be like that? My staff didn't appreciate how hard I worked and how much I did.

Use formal assessment procedures with your staff. Administer all or parts of the McEwan Instructional Leadership Behavioral Checklist to some or all of your staff members. Discuss the results with your leadership team and use them to plan improvement initiatives.

Work (network) with colleagues. The most exciting thing about preparing this manuscript was reading the questionnaires and talking with the dozens of instructional leaders who assisted me. They are an impressive and awe-inspiring group of individuals. People like them work in every community and state. Talk to them, shadow them, and pick their brains at every opportunity. Join state and national professional organizations and volunteer for committees.

Attend classes. Begin to work on an advanced degree. Roland Barth chides principals not to become the at-risk principal, who, like the at-risk student, "leaves school before or after graduation with little possibility of continuing learning."[1] While every class *won't* inspire you, the contacts with other educators, the opportunities for thinking and reading, and the challenge of being a learner yourself *will*. Spend part of every summer in a professional institute experience. Many instructional leaders have attended the Harvard Principals Center or a Scholars Seminar at NAESP or NASSP with astounding results in their personal and professional lives.

Read books. You may already have an advanced degree, but that shouldn't keep you from learning. Become a student of the leadership literature. Find out what Bennis, Covey, Glickman, Goodlad, and others are thinking and writing about. Their ideas can't help but inspire you.

Subscribe to journals and newspapers and read them. My favorites are *Education Week, Educational Leadership, NASSP Bulletin, Principal,* and *Phi Delta Kappan.*

Set goals. If you're not setting short-term, long-term, and visionary goals in all areas of your life—work, educational, family, social, and spiritual, you're missing out on some real benefits in your life. In its Aspiring Principals Workshop, the National Association of Elementary School Principals emphasizes the following benefits of setting goals:

- Break out of that "being in a rut" feeling.
- Reduce the frequency of down days.
- Help stretch peak days.
- Tap unused potential.
- Stretch thinking.
- Reduce procrastination.
- Develop a winning attitude.
- Rediscover optimism.
- Make better use of your subconscious.
- Become more self-motivated.

The Principal's Lament

I am all things
to all good men,
My gut doth wrench;
my heart doth pound.
I meet myself coming and
going again
To emergency duties—the
crises abound.
Instructional leadership's my
calling, you see,
I give it my best, I'm blazing
that trail;
When daily routine gets the
best of me,
I accomplish that well, to
no avail.
Like milkweed it grows, or
a well-watered flower,
It consumes the spirit,
it drains the soul;
As Sisyphus, when, with
each passing hour,
Plods helplessly on
from the loftiest goal.
I'll visit a class on that rare
stellar day,
No longer a stranger; no
more Sturm und Drang;
My diogenic lamp will light
up the way,
Not with a whimper—
a primordial bang.
To be free, to soar to that
precipice high,
Where efficacy reigns, the
thrill returns;
The teacher is "bubbling,"
the minutes race by;
Attentions are rapt,
the students do learn.
So now I'm off to the
instructional fray,
My empowerment real,
it is a fact;
I'll visit those classrooms
the rest of the day,
But first a few matters to
which I react.
I pick up the phone and
babble, some say,
I feel like Prometheus
bound;
Chained to the desk and
out of the way,
An occasional rustle, a
slight clanking sound.
It needn't be thus,
there must be a way!
Rise up! Be strong! Complain!
Demand that instruction be
part of each day.
Time lost one can never regain!

James A. Blockinger

Take risks. I've taken some big ones in my day. I volunteered to bring a teacher and her class to be observed by 125 other administrators and then agreed to conduct a conference with her in front of them. I challenged a local businessman to trade places with me for a day. Although the adage says "think before you act," there are many occasions when we ponder too long over the ramifications of something and fail to seize the moment.

Volunteer to teach a class or workshop. Jim Blockinger has taught Administrators' Academies in supervision and instructional leadership. Although Jim's academies have helped countless Illinois administrators to improve, no one has improved more from his classes than Jim.

Join professional organizations and become active. Become affiliated with the National Association of Elementary School Principals, the National Association of Secondary School Principals, or the Association for Supervision and Curriculum Development. Join the state affiliates of these organizations as well. Attend meetings, and volunteer for committees. Rubbing shoulders with other instructional leaders in your state and nation will enlarge your horizons and expand your vision.

Think and reflect on your own practice of the principalship. If you are moving through your work without constant reflection on all of the things that are happening, you are missing out on wonderful learning opportunities.

Effective instructional leaders are never satisfied. They always want more—from themselves, from their teachers, and from their students. They are learning something new every day. They know they can't expect their teachers to give them more than they themselves are willing to give, and they're constantly aware that everyone is watching to see if they're "walking their talk."

"[What we need to do is] turn the reflection of the school principal to the core technology of schooling—teaching and learning—and achieve the same level of reflection on curriculum, program development, and instruction that may well already go on with less important or critical matters."

Wilma Smith and Richard Andrews

"The first step toward effectiveness is to decide what are the right things to do. Efficiency, which is doing things right, is irrelevant until you work on the right things."

Peter Drucker

Many instructional leaders have had to learn patience. Although they are motivated, driven to accomplish what they know needs to be done, and have a vision for the future, they recognize the folly of bulldozing a plan. Nancy Carbone explains it in this way: "You have to believe in the process and have patience with people." She elaborates, "I found that if I presented the information for people in a variety of ways and trusted their instincts to do the right thing, they would not disappoint me." Instructional leaders have also learned that their work is never really done. For task-oriented individuals who want to cross things off their proverbial lists, instructional leadership means never being finished. Alan Jones summarized it neatly when he said, "You really need patience. Profound change takes five to seven years. Change is not a rational process. You just have to have a vision and then hang on for the ride!"

> "Renewal is the principle—and the process—that empowers us to move on an upward spiral of growth and change, on continuous improvement."
>
> Stephen R. Covey

Challenge for the Future

Begin today to change some of the ways you do business in your school. The research is clear. How you act every day makes a difference in the educational lives of students. Through the words you use, the actions you choose, and the vision you pursue, you will make a major impact on student learning. The question is—What kind of an impact are you making as an instructional leader? Altering even a few instructional leadership behaviors will produce dramatic results in the effectiveness of your teachers, the learning of students, and the personal satisfaction you'll feel from having made a difference.

Note

1. Dennis Sparks, "The Professional Development of Principals: A Conversation with Roland Barth," *Journal of Staff Development* (Winter, 1993): 19.

References for Quotations

Chapter One

Warren Bennis and Burt Nanus, *Leaders: The Strategies for Taking Charge* (New York: Harper & Row Publishers, 1985), 223.

Richard Andrews and Richard Soder, "Principal Leadership and Student Achievement," *Educational Leadership* (March 1987): 9.

Thomas B. Greenfield, "Leaders and Schools: Willfulness and Non-Natural Order in Organizations," in *Leadership and Organizational Culture,* Thomas J. Sergiovanni and John E. Corbally, eds. (Urbana-Champaign: University of Illinois Press, 1984), 509.

Warren Bennis, *On Becoming a Leader* (Reading, Massachusetts: Addison-Wesley Publishing Company, Inc., 1989), 45.

Niccolo Machiavelli, *The Prince,* Harvey C. Mansfield, Jr., trans. (Chicago, Illinois: University of Chicago Press, 1985), 23.

Keith Acheson and Stuart C. Smith, *It Is Time for Principals to Share the Responsibility for Instructional Leadership With Others* (Eugene, Oregon: Oregon School Study Council, February 1986), 3.

Phillip C. Schlechty, *Schools for the 21st Century* (San Francisco: Jossey-Bass Publishers, 1990), xix.

Chapter Two

James R. Weber, *Instructional Leadership: A Composite Working Model* (Eugene, Oregon: ERIC Clearinghouse on Educational Management, 1987), 6.

Roland Barth, *Run School Run* (Cambridge, Massachusetts: Harvard University Press, 1980), 97.

United States Department of Education, *What Works: Research About Teaching and Learning* (Washington, D.C.: United States Department of Education, 1986), 45.

John Jay Bonstingl, *Schools of Quality: An Introduction to Total Quality Management in Education* (Alexandria, Virginia: Association for Supervision and Curriculum Development, 1992), 78.

Lawrence W. Lezotte, *Creating the Total Quality Effective School* (Okemos, Michigan: Effective Schools Products, Ltd., 1992), 58.

Richard P. DuFour and Robert Eaker, *Fulfilling the Promise of Excellence: A Practitioner's Guide to School Improvement* (Westbury, New York: J. L. Wilkerson Publishing Company, 1989), 158-59.

Chapter Three

Tom Peters and Nancy Austin, *A Passion for Excellence: The Leadership Difference* (New York: Random House, 1985), 264.

United States Department of Education, *What Works: Research About Teaching and Learning* (Washington, D.C.: United States Department of Education, 1986), 51.

Field Marshal Bernard Montgomery, quoted in Tom Peters and Nancy Austin, *A Passion for Excellence: The Leadership Difference*, (New York: Random House, 1985), 264.

Aristotle, *The Metaphysics Books I-IX* (Book I), Hugh Tredennick, trans. (Cambridge, Massachusetts: Harvard University Press, 1933), 3.

Arthur G. Powell, Eleanor Farrar, and David K. Cohen, *The Shopping Mall High School: Winners and Losers in the Educational Marketplace* (Boston: Houghton Mifflin Company, 1985), 320.

Roland Barth, *Run School Run* (Cambridge, Massachusetts: Harvard University Press, 1980), 171.

Bruce Joyce and Beverly Showers, *Student Achievement Through Staff Development* (New York: Longman, 1988), 21.

Chapter Four

Richard Andrews, "The Illinois Principal as Instructional Leader: A Concept and Definition Paper," *Illinois Principal* (March 1989): 4.

Jeannie Oakes, *Keeping Track: How Schools Structure Inequality* (New Haven, Connecticut: Yale University Press, 1985), 7.

William Gauthier, Jr., "Focusing for Effectiveness," *Choices* (October 1980): 16-17.

Charles W. Eliot,"Shortening and Enriching the Grammar School Course," in *Charles W. Eliot and Popular Education,* E.A.Krug, ed. (New York: Teachers' College Press, 1961), 52-53.

Terrence Deal, "The Symbolism of Effective Schools," *Elementary School Journal,* Vol. 85. No. 5 (1985): 601-20.

Terrence E. Deal and Allen A. Kennedy, *Corporate Cultures: The Rites and Rituals of Corporate Life* (Reading, Massachusetts: Addison-Wesley Publishing Company, 1982), 23.

Scott Thompson in Edgar A. Kelly, *Improving School Climate* (Reston, Virginia: National Association of Secondary School Principals, 1970), v.

John Goodlad in Mary Anne Raywid, Charles Tesconie, and Donald Warren, *Pride and Promise: Schools of Excellence for All People* (Westbury, New York: American Educational Studies Association, 1985), 14.

Chapter Five

Thomas J. Sergiovanni, "Leadership and Excellence in Schooling," *Educational Leadership* (February 1984): 9.

James R. Weber, *Instructional Leadership: Contexts and Challenges* (Eugene, Oregon: Oregon School Study Council, 1987), 13.

Charles Garfield, *Peak Performers: The New Heroes of American Business* (New York: William Morrow and Company, Inc., 1986), 96.

Karl Weick, "Administering Education in Loosely Coupled Schools," *Phi Delta Kappan* (June 1982): 675.

Chapter Six

Keith Acheson, *The Principal's Role in Instructional Leadership* (Eugene, Oregon: Oregon School Study Council, 1985), 1.

Carl Rogers, "In Retrospect — Forty-Six Years," *American Psychologist* (1974): 115.

Albert Shanker in Terrence Deal, "The Culture of Schools," in *Leadership: Examining the Elusive,* Linda T. Sheive and Marian B. Schoenheit, eds. (Alexandria, Virginia: Association for Supervision and Curriculum Development, 1987), 3.

Thomas D. Bird and Judith Warren Little, *Instructional Leadership in Eight Secondary Schools. Final Report* (Boulder, Colorado: Center for Action Research, Inc., 1985).

Chapter Seven

Carl Glickman, "Pretending Not to Know What We Know," *Educational Leadership* (May 1991): 7.

Michael Fullan, "Visions that Blind," *Educational Leadership* (February 1992): 19.

Edward Pajak, "Change and Continuity in Supervision and Leadership," in *Challenges and Achievements of American Education* (Alexandria, Virginia: Association for Supervision and Curriculum Development, 1993), 178.

Thomas J. Sergiovanni, "On Rethinking Leadership: A Conversation with Tom Sergiovanni," *Educational Leadership* (February 1992): 48.

Samuel B. Bacharach, "The Balance of Power," *Education Week* (February 1993): 14.

Seymour B. Sarason, *The Predictable Failure of Educational Reform: Can We Change Course Before It's Too Late?* (San Francisco: Jossey-Bass Publishers, 1990), 61.

Chapter Eight

David W. Johnson and Rogert T. Johnson, *Leading the Cooperative School* (Edina, Minnesota: Interaction Book Company, 1989), 1.

Sara Lawrence Lightfoot, *The Good High School* (New York: Basic Books, Inc., Publishers, 1983), 25.

Richard D. Sagor, "Three Principals Who Make a Difference," *Educational Leadership* (February 1992): 18.

Stephen R. Covey, *The Seven Habits of Highly Effective People: Restoring the Character Ethic* (New York: Simon & Schuster, 1989), 264.

Chapter Nine

Joel Barker, *Future Edge: Discovering the New Paradigms of Success* (New York: William Morrow and Company, Inc., 1992), 21.

Max DePree, *Leadership Is an Art* (New York: Doubleday, 1989), 49.

Phillip Schlechty, *Schools for the 21st Century: Leadership Imperatives for Educational Reform* (San Francisco: Jossey-Bass Publishers, 1991), 98.

John Goodlad, *A Place Called School: Prospects for the Future* (New York: McGraw-Hill Book Company, 1984), 321.

Warren Bennis, *On Becoming a Leader* (Reading, Massachusetts: Addison-Wesley Publishing Co., Inc., 1989), 3.

James A. Blockinger is superintendent of schools in Millburn C. C. School District, Wadsworth, Illinois. He is a former middle-level and high-school administrator. This poem was first published in *NASSP Bulletin*/September 1992, page 81.

Wilma Smith and Richard Andrews, *Instructional Leadership: How Principals Make a Difference* (Alexandria, Virginia: Association for Curriculum and Supervision, 1989), 4.

Peter Drucker, *Managing the Nonprofit Organization: Principles and Practices* (New York: HarperCollins Publishers, 1990), 198.

Stephen R. Covey, *The Seven Habits of Highly Successful People : Restoring the Character Ethic* (New York: Simon & Schuster, Inc., 1989), 304.

Bibliography

Acheson, Keith. *The Principal's Role in Instructional Leadership.* Eugene, Oregon: Oregon School Study Council, 1985.

Acheson, Keith, and Stuart C. Smith. *It Is Time for Principals to Share the Responsibility for Instructional Leadership With Others.* Eugene, Oregon: Oregon School Study Council (February 1986):Volume 29, No. 6.

Andrews, Richard. "The Illinois Principal as Instructional Leader." *Illinois Principal* (March 1989): 4-12.

Andrews, Richard, and Roger Soder. "Principal Leadership and Student Achievement." *Educational Leadership* (March 1987): 9-11.

Barker, Joel. *Future Edge: Discovering the New Paradigms of Success.* New York: William Morrow and Company, Inc., 1991.

Barth, Roland. *Run School Run.* Cambridge, Massachusetts: Harvard University Press, 1980.

Bass, B. "Effects of the Nature of the Problem on LGD Performance." *Journal of Applied Psychology, 37* (1953): 96-99.

Bennis, Warren. *On Becoming a Leader.* Reading, Massachusetts: Addison-Wesley Publishing Company, Inc., 1989.

Bennis, Warren. "Transformation Power and Leadership." In *Leadership and Organizational Culture.* Thomas J. Sergiovanni and John E. Corbally, eds. Urbana-Champaign: University of Illinois Press, 1984.

Bennis, Warren, and Burt Nanus. *Leaders: The Strategies for Taking Charge.* New York: Harper & Row, 1985.

Bird, Thomas D., and Judith Warren Little. *Instructional Leadership in Eight Secondary Schools. Final Report.* Boulder, Colorado: Center for Action Research, Inc., 1985.

Bonstingl, John Jay. *Schools of Quality: An Introduction to Total Quality Management in Education.* Alexandria, Virginia: Association for Supervision and Curriculum Development, 1992.

Cawelti, Gordon, ed. *Challenges and Achievements of American Education.* Alexandria, Virginia: Association for Curriuculum and Supervision, 1993.

Covey, Stephen R. *The Seven Habits of Highly Effective People: Restoring the Character Ethic.* New York: Simon & Schuster, 1989.

Curwin, Richard L., and Allen N. Mendler. *Discipline With Dignity.* Alexandria, Virginia: Association for Supervision and Curriculum Development, 1988.

Deal, Terrence E., and Allan A. Kennedy. *Corporate Cultures: The Rites and Rituals of Corporate Life.* Reading, Massachusetts: Addison-Wesley Publishing Company, 1982.

DuFour, Richard P. *The Principal as Staff Developer.* Bloomington, Indiana: National Education Service, 1991.

DuFour, Richard P., and Robert Eaker. *Creating the New American School: A Principal's Guide to School Improvement.* Bloomington, Indiana: National Education Service, 1992.

DuFour, Richard P., and Robert Eaker. *Fulfilling the Promise of Excellence: A Practitioner's Guide to School Improvement.* Westbury, New York: J. L. Wilkerson Publishing Company, 1989.

Garfield, Charles. *Peak Performers: The New Heroes of American Business.* New York: William Morrow and Company, Inc., 1986.

Glickman, Carl., ed. *Supervision in Transition.* Alexandria, Virginia: Association for Supervision and Curriculum Development, 1992.

Good, Thomas L. "Teacher Expectations and Student Perceptions: A Decade of Research." *Educational Leadership.* (February, 1981): 415-22.

Goodlad, John I. *A Place Called School: Prospects for the Future.* New York: McGraw-Hill Book Company, 1984.

Howard, Eugene, Bruce Howell, and Edward Brainard. *Handbook for Conducting School Climate Improvement Projects.* Bloomington, Indiana: Phi Delta Kappa Educational Foundation, 1987.

Illinois State Board of Education. *The Principal as Instructional Leader: A Research Synthesis.* Monograph #1. Springfield, Illinois: Illinois State Board of Education, 1986.

Johnson, David W., and Roger T. Johnson. *Leading the Cooperative School.* Edina, Minnesota: Interaction Book Company, 1989.

Joyce, Bruce, and Beverly Showers. *Student Achievement Through Staff Development*. New York: Longman, 1988.

Kerman, Sam. "Teacher Expectations and Student Achievement." *Phi Delta Kappan* (June 1979): 716-18.

Lasley, Thomas J., and William W. Wayson. "Characteristics of Schools with Good Discipline." *Educational Leadership* (December 1982): 28-31.

Lezotte, Lawrence W. *Creating the Total Quality Effective School*. Okemos, Michigan: Effective Schools Products, Ltd., 1992.

Lightfoot, Sara Lawrence. *The Good High School*. New York: Basic Books, Inc., Publishers, 1983.

Linn, Eleanor, and Norma Barquet. "Assessing the Tracking Practices in Your School." *Equity Coalition*. Ann Arbor, Michigan: Programs for Educational Opportunity (Autumn, 1992): 16-17.

Mahaffy, John E. *Collegial Support System: A Process Model Draft*. A paper prepared for the Northwest Regional Educational Laboratory. Portland, Oregon: Northwest Regional Educational Laboratory, 1988.

Mazzarella, Jo Ann. *Instructional Leadership: Profile of an Elementary School Principal*. Eugene, Oregon: Oregon School Study Council (November 1982): Volume 26, No.3.

Mazzarella, Jo Ann. *Instructional Leadership: Profile of a High School Principal*. Eugene, Oregon: Oregon School Study Council (January 1983): Volume 26, No. 5.

Murphy, Joseph, Marsha Weil, Philip Hallinger, and Alexis Mitman. "Academic Press: Translating High Expectations Into School Policies and Classroom Practices." *Educational Leadership* (December 1982): 22-26.

National Association of Elementary School Principals. *Proficiencies for Principals*. Alexandria, Virginia: National Association of Elementary School Principals, 1986.

Oakes, Jeannie. *Keeping Track: How Schools Structure Inequality*. New Haven, Connecticut: Yale University Press, 1985.

Peters, Tom, and Nancy Austin. *A Passion for Excellence: The Leadership Difference*. New York: Random House, 1985.

Peters, Thomas J., and Robert H. Waterman, Jr. *In Search of Excellence: Lessons from America's Best-Run Companies*. New York: Harper & Row Publishers, 1982.

Purkey, William Watson. *Inviting School Success: A Self-Concept Approach to Teaching and Learning*. Belmont, California: Wadsworth Publishing Co., Inc., 1978.

Russell, James S., Jo Ann Mazzarella, Thomas White, and Steven Maurer. *Linking the Behaviors and Activities of Secondary School Principals to School Effectiveness: A Focus on Effective and Ineffective Behaviors*. Eugene, Oregon: Center for Educational Policy and Management, 1985.

Saphier, Jon, and Robert Gower. *The Skillful Teacher: Building Your Teaching Skills*. Carlisle, Massachusetts: Research for Better Teaching, Inc., 1987.

Schlechty, Phillip C. *Schools for the 21st Century: Leadership Imperatives for Educational Reform*. San Francisco: Jossey-Bass Publishers, 1990.

Sergiovanni, Thomas J. "Leadership and Excellence in Schooling." *Educational Leadership* (February 1984): 4-13.

Sergiovanni, Thomas J. *The Principalship: A Reflective Practice Perspective*. Boston: Allyn and Bacon, Inc., 1987.

Sheive, Linda T., and Marian B. Schoenheit, eds. *Leadership: Examining the Elusive*. Alexandria, Virginia: Association for Supervision and Curriculum Development, 1987.

Smith, Stuart C., and Philip K. Piele, eds. *School Leadership: Handbook for Excellence*. Eugene, Oregon: ERIC Clearinghouse on Educational Management, 1989.

Smith, Wilma F., and Richard L. Andrews. *Instructional Leadership: How Principals Make a Difference*. Alexandria, Virginia: Association for Supervision and Curriculum Development, 1989.

United States Department of Education. *What Works: Research About Teaching and Learning*. Washington, D.C.: United States Department of Education, 1986.

Weber, James R. *Instructional Leadership: A Composite Working Model*. Eugene, Oregon: ERIC Clearinghouse on Educational Management, 1987.

Weber, James R. *Instructional Leadership: Contexts and Challenges*. Eugene, Oregon: Oregon School Study Council, 1987.

Weber, James R. *Models of Instructional Leadership: Annotated Bibliography*. Eugene, Oregon: ERIC Clearinghouse on Educational Management, 1987.

Complete Instructional Leadership Behavioral Checklist and Response Form

Establish and implement instructional goals

Indicator 1.1 Involves teachers in developing and implementing school instructional goals and objectives

Comment:

The main focus of Indicator 1.1 is the involvement of teachers with the principal in the development and implementation of instructional goals and objectives.

SCALE OF DESCRIPTORS:

1. Curriculum is textbook driven, and neither principal nor teachers have involvement in the development of instructional goals.

2. Principal makes all decisions regarding instructional goals and objectives with no input from faculty.

3. Faculty input is solicited and/or received from time to time, but no organized system for developing instructional goals is in place, and unilateral decisions regarding curricula are frequently made.

4. Principal and faculty have worked together in a systematic fashion to establish achievement objectives (learner outcomes), but implementation of objectives is an individual classroom activity.

5. Principal and faculty have jointly established specific achievement objectives, and faculty members share responsibility for the buildingwide implementation of these objectives.

KEY POINTS IN DESCRIPTORS:

1. No involvement of either teachers or principal

2. No involvement of teachers

3. Minimal involvement of teachers

4. Joint involvement of teachers and principal in development

5. Joint involvement of teachers and principal in development and implcmcntation

Indicator 1.2 Incorporates the designated state and/or system curricula in the development of instructional programs

Comment:

The main focus of Indicator 1.2 is the support the principal gives to mandated state and local programs while designing an instructional program that meets the needs of the individual school and/or classroom.

SCALE OF DESCRIPTORS:

1. Principal does not support the incorporation of state and/or system curricula into the instructional program.

2. Principal feels that state and/or system curricula should be included in the instructional program but permits teachers to exercise personal judgments regarding their ultimate inclusion.

3. Principal feels that state and/or system curricula should be included and communicates these expectations to teachers.

4. Principal feels that state and/or system curricula should be included, communicates these expectations to teachers, and works with them in the development of instructional programs that do this effectively.

5. Principal feels that state and/or system curricula should be included, communicates these expectations to teachers, works with them in the development of instructional programs that do this effectively, and monitors classroom activities to ensure such inclusion.

KEY POINTS IN DESCRIPTORS:

1. No incorporation of state or system curricula into program

2. Belief in importance but permissive in supervision

3. Belief in importance with expectations communicated

4. Belief in importance, expectations communicated, assistance provided

5. Belief in importance, expectations communicated, assistance provided, and implementation monitored

Indicator 1.3 Ensures that school and classroom activities are consistent with school instructional goals and objectives

Comment:

The main focus of Indicator 1.3 is the match between instructional goals and what is happening in individual classrooms and the school as a whole, and what the principal is doing to ensure that consistency exists throughout the building. The existence of clear instructional goals is a given in this indicator.

SCALE OF DESCRIPTORS:

1. Although school instructional goals and objectives do exist, many activities appear to act as deterrents and/or impediments to the achievement of goals and objectives.

2. Although school instructional goals and objectives do exist, activities in the school as a whole (majority of classrooms) do not appear to support these objectives.

3. Although activities in the school as a whole appear to support the stated instructional goals and objectives, there are many individual classrooms in which activities do not support school goals.

4. Activities in most classrooms and the school as a whole appear to support the stated instructional goals and objectives.

5. Activities in all classrooms and the school as a whole appear to support the stated instructional goals and objectives.

KEY POINTS IN DESCRIPTORS:

1. Principal is unwilling to address a lack of consistency in *many* classrooms (more than half) or in the *school as a whole.*

2. Principal expresses a verbal willingness to address lack of consistency but fails to follow through with actions to ensure consistency.

3. Principal is willing to address a lack of consistency between goals and activities but is marginally effective in doing so.

4. Principal is willing to ensure consistency between goals and activities and is usually very effective in doing so.

5. Principal is highly effective in ensuring that activities match objectives.

Indicator 1.4 Evaluates progress toward instructional goals and objectives

Comment:

The main focus of Indicator 1.4 is the use of a combination of evaluation methods, and if needed, subsequent adjustments in program to ensure that goals and objectives are being met.

SCALE OF DESCRIPTORS:

1. No schoolwide program of testing exists.

2. Although a schoolwide standardized testing program exists, this information is used in a general systemwide way, and the principal does not use the information to evaluate the school program.

3. Standardized test information is the sole indicator used by the principal for program evaluation. Review of the information is not systematic or specific, and teachers rarely review the results beyond the initial report.

4. The results of multiple-assessment methods such as mastery skills checklists, criterion-referenced tests, standardized tests, and performance or portfolio assessments are systematically used and reviewed by the principal along with teachers.

5. Results of multiple-assessment methods are systematically used to evaluate program objectives. Teachers and principals analyze the results and together make program modifications.

KEY POINTS IN DESCRIPTORS:

1. No standardized testing program

2. Standardized testing program with little utilization of results by either principal or teachers

3. Standardized testing program with some utilization of results by principal and little utilization of results by teachers

4. Well-rounded evaluation program with some utilization of results by both principal and teachers

5. Well-rounded evaluation program with effective utilization of results by both principal and teachers to modify and improve program

STEP TWO: **Be there for your staff.**

Indicator 2.1 Works with teachers to improve the instructional program in their classrooms consistent with student needs

Comment:

The main focus of Indicator 2.1 is the role of the principal as an instructional resource person for teachers. Quality and quantity of assistance are to be considered as well as the frequency with which teachers call on the principal for assistance.

SCALE OF DESCRIPTORS:

1. Principal has no interaction with teachers regarding the instructional program in their classrooms. Principal has almost no understanding of instructional program. Teachers never ask for instructional assistance from the principal, preferring to deal with instructional matters independently.

2. Principal rarely assists teachers with instructional concerns but will attempt to assist a teacher if a specific, well-defined request is made. Principal has very sketchy knowledge and understanding of the instructional program. Few requests are made by teachers for assistance.

3. Principal works in a limited way with those few teachers who request help. Principal's knowledge of instructional strategies is basic, and outside resources are often needed to solve instructional problems.

4. Principal works with most teachers through coordination and delegation, showing a strong degree of expertise. Teachers frequently turn to the principal for assistance.

5. Principal works with all teachers on a continuing basis and is an important resource for instructional concerns. Interaction is frequently initiated by the principal, and teachers regularly turn to the principal for help, which they receive with a high level of expertise.

KEY POINTS IN DESCRIPTORS:

1. No interaction, no expertise, no requests for assistance

2. Little interaction, limited expertise, few requests for assistance

3. Some interaction, basic expertise, some requests for assistance

4. Frequent interaction, strong expertise, frequent requests for assistance

5. Regular interaction, outstanding expertise, regular requests for assistance

Indicator 2.2 Bases instructional program development on sound research and practice

155

Comment:

The main focus of Indicator 2.2 is the status of the principal as an active learner in the acquisition of current educational research and practice, and how effectively this knowledge base is shared and translated into instructional programs.

SCALE OF DESCRIPTORS:

1. Principal is unaware of current educational research and practice.

2. Principal is aware of current educational research and practice but feels this body of knowledge has little bearing on the day-to-day functioning of the school.

3. Principal is aware of current educational research and practice and believes it should affect program development but is not currently attempting to translate this information into practice.

4. Principal is aware of current educational research and practice, believes it should affect program development, shares it actively with staff, and is currently attempting to translate this information into instructional program development.

5. Principal is aware of current educational research and practice, believes it should affect program development, shares it actively with staff, and has successfully developed and/or altered school programs to reflect this knowledge base.

KEY POINTS IN DESCRIPTORS:

1. No awareness of or belief in the importance or use of current educational research

2. Some awareness of but no belief in importance or use of current educational research

3. Some awareness of and belief in importance but no use of current educational research

4. Awareness of and belief in importance, some attempts to translate information into instructional program

5 Awareness of and belief in importance, successful implementation of school programs based on research

Indicator 2.3 Applies appropriate formative procedures in evaluating the instructional program

Comment:

The main focus of Indicator 2.3 is the combination of multiple methods of evaluation that are formative in nature and allow for immediate adjustments in instructional strategies, groupings, time allocations, and lesson design.

Examples of formative evaluation tools are teacher-made tests, samples of student work, mastery skills checklists, criterion-referenced tests, end-of-unit tests, and so on.

SCALE OF DESCRIPTORS:

1. Principal does not receive any regular formative evaluation information from classroom teachers.

2. Principal receives some formative evaluation information from some classroom teachers, but sharing of this information is voluntary.

3. Principal solicits some formative evaluation information regularly from all classroom teachers.

4. Principal solicits some formative evaluation information regularly from all classroom teachers and discusses this information with teachers.

5. Principal solicits complete formative evaluation information regularly from all classroom teachers, discusses this information with teachers, and together with teachers plans for changes in day-to-day classroom practices.

KEY POINTS IN DESCRIPTORS:

1. No regular formative evaluation information

2. Some voluntary formative evaluation information

3. Formative evaluation information solicited regularly

4. Formative evaluation information solicited regularly and discussed

5. Formative evaluation information solicited regularly, discussed, and instructional practices adjusted

STEP THREE: **Create a school culture and climate conducive to learning.**

Indicator 3.1 Establishes high expectations for student achievement that are directly communicated to students, teachers, and parents

Comment:

The main focus of Indicator 3.1 is the philosophical assumptions the individual makes about the ability of all students to learn, the need for both equity and excellence in the educational program, and the ability to communicate these beliefs to students, teachers, and parents.

SCALE OF DESCRIPTORS:

1. Principal believes that nonalterable variables such as home background, socioeconomic status, and ability level are the prime determinants of student achievement and that the school cannot overcome these factors.

2. Principal believes that the nonalterable variables cited above significantly affect student achievement and that the school has a limited impact on student achievement.

3. Principal believes that although the nonalterable variables cited above may influence student achievement, teachers are responsible for all students mastering basic skills/prescribed learner outcomes according to individual levels of expectancy. The principal occasionally communicates these expectations in an informal way to students, teachers, and parents via written and spoken communications and/or specific activities.

4. Principal believes that although the nonalterable variables cited above may influence student achievement, teachers are responsible for all students mastering certain basic skills at their grade level and frequently communicates these expectations to teachers, parents, and students in a formal, organized manner. Expectations for student achievement may be communicated through written statements of objectives in basic skills and/or a written statement of purpose/mission for the school that guides the instructional program.

5. Principal believes that together the home and school can have a profound influence on student achievement. Teachers are held responsible not only for all students mastering certain basic skills at their grade level but for the stimulation, enrichment, and acceleration of the student who is able to learn more quickly and the provision of extended learning opportunities for students who may need more time for mastery. Expectations for student achievement are developed jointly among students, teachers, and parents and are communicated not only through written statements of learner outcomes in core curriculum areas but in enriched and accelerated programs, achievement awards, and opportunities for creative expression.

KEY POINTS IN DESCRIPTORS:

1. No impact by school on students; no communication of achievement expectations to students, teachers, or parents

2. Limited impact by school on students; no communication of achievement expectations to students, teachers, or parents

3. All students should master basic learner outcomes; limited communication of achievement expectations to students, teachers, and parents

4. All students should master basic learner outcomes; formal communication of achievement expectations to students, teachers, and parents

5. All students master basic learner outcomes with many students exceeding the minimal competencies, participating in enriched or accelerated course, and receiving academic awards; joint development of achievement expectations by students, teachers, and parents

Indicator 3.2 Establishes clear rules and expectations for the use of time allocated to instruction and monitors the effective use of classroom time

Comment:

The main focus of Indicator 3.2 is the existence of written guidelines for use of classroom time, the existence of a weekly program schedule for each classroom teacher, the regular monitoring of lesson plans, and the schoolwide schedule and its impact on instructional time.

SCALE OF DESCRIPTORS:

1. Teachers are totally unsupervised in the planning of their daily schedule. No written guidelines exist for the use of classroom time. There are frequent interruptions that significantly interfere with instruction.

2. State, district, or school guidelines for the use of classroom time exist, but the principal does not monitor their implementation in the classroom. There are many interruptions to instructional time that could be avoided.

3. State, district, or school guidelines for the use of classroom time exist, and the principal monitors their implementation in the classroom by requiring teachers to post a copy of their weekly schedule and by occasionally reviewing lesson plans. There are regular but infrequent interruptions on a planned basis.

4. State, district, or school guidelines for the use of classroom time exist, and the principal monitors their implementation by requiring teachers to post a weekly program schedule and regularly reviewing lesson plans. Basic skill instructional time is occasionally interrupted with advance notice. Whenever possible, interruptions are planned during noninstructional time.

5. State, district, or school guidelines for the use of classroom time exist, and the principal regularly monitors their implementation through the review of classroom or grade level lesson plans and regular classroom visitations. Classroom instructional time is rarely interrupted, and the principal plans with teachers the coordination of schoolwide schedules to minimize the effect of pull-out programs, assemblies, and other special events.

KEY POINTS IN DESCRIPTORS:

1. No guidelines

2. Guidelines, no monitoring, frequent interruptions

3. Guidelines, limited monitoring, limited interruptions

4. Guidelines, frequent monitoring, few interruptions

5. Guidelines, frequent monitoring, coordinated school schedule to minimize interruptions

---

Indicator 3.3 Establishes, implements, and evaluates with teachers and students (as appropriate) procedures and codes for handling and correcting discipline problems

---

Comment:

The main focus in Indicator 3.3 is the existence of a discipline plan for each classroom and for the building as a whole, and the participation of the principal in the implementation of this plan. The focus of the plan is on responsible, caring behavior by all students and teachers based on mutual respect and common goals. Positive as well as negative reinforcers are included in the plan.

SCALE OF DESCRIPTORS:

1. Each classroom teacher has his or her own method of handling discipline problems without support or assistance from the principal, and there is no schoolwide discipline plan or comprehensive set of school rules.

2. Each classroom teacher has his or her own method of handling discipline, and no schoolwide discipline plan or set of school rules exists. The principal is available for assistance with

severe discipline problems and handles them on an individual basis with little uniformity or consistency.

3. Each classroom teacher files a discipline plan with the principal, and rules for behavior in common areas of the building are available. The principal is generally supportive and provides assistance with discipline problems.

4. Each classroom teacher files a discipline plan with the principal. Rules for student behavior in common areas of the building have been developed jointly by the principal/teachers/students (as appropriate) and made available to all parents and students. The principal is consistent and cooperative in implementing school discipline.

5. In addition to individual classroom discipline plans and rules for student behavior in common areas of the building, a buildingwide discipline plan has been developed in which the principal assumes a joint responsibility with all staff members, students, and parents for discipline and school behavior. A climate of mutual respect exists among students, teachers, and the principal based on the fair application of the plan.

KEY POINTS IN DESCRIPTORS:

1. No classroom plans, no school rules, no schoolwide plan, no principal support

2. No classroom plans, no school rules, no schoolwide plan, some principal support

3. Classroom plans, school rules, no schoolwide plan, adequate principal support

4. Classroom plans, school rules developed jointly and furnished to students and parents, no schoolwide plan, and excellent principal support

5. Classroom plans, school rules developed jointly and furnished to students and parents, schoolwide plan developed jointly and furnished to students and parents, excellent principal support

STEP FOUR: Communicate the vision and mission of your school to students, staff, and parents.

Indicator 4.1 Provides for systematic two-way communication with staff regarding the ongoing objectives and goals of the school

Comment:

The main focus of Indicator 4.1 is the provision of two-way communications channels to ensure an ongoing discussion of the mission of the school.

SCALE OF DESCRIPTORS:

1. There is no communication between principal and staff regarding the mission of the school.

2. Communication between principal and staff is largely one-way and limited to administrative directives regarding principal expectations.

3. Although principal and staff communicate informally regarding the mission of the school, there are no regular two-way communications channels.

4. Two-way communications channels between principal and staff have been established in the form of faculty meetings, grade level/departmental/team meetings, and teacher/principal conferences, but these channels are frequently used for administrative or social purposes and are not regularly devoted to a discussion of instructional goals and priorities.

5. Established two-way communications channels are regularly used by the principal as a means of conveying the goals and objectives of the school to the staff.

KEY POINTS IN DESCRIPTORS:

1. No communication

2. One-way communication, no established channels

3. Informal two-way communication, no established channels

4. Established channels, no regular use of these channels

5. Regular use of established channels for two-way communication regarding school mission

Indicator 4.2 Establishes, supports, and implements activities that communicate to students the value and meaning of learning

Comment:

The main focus of Indicator 4.2 is the existence of activities that communicate the value of learning to students. Examples of such activities might be awards or honors assemblies, learning incentive programs, career awareness programs, honor societies, work/study programs, academic clubs, and mentoring or shadowing programs. This list is meant to be prescriptive but certainly not inclusive.

1. No activities exist that communicate the value and meaning of learning to students

2. At least one activity exists that communicates the value and meaning of learning to students

3. More than three activities exist that communicate the value and meaning of learning to students

4. More than six activities exist that communicate the value and meaning of learning to students

5. More than ten activities exist that communicate the value and meaning of learning to students

KEY POINTS IN DESCRIPTORS:

1. No activities

2. One activity

3. More than three activities

4. More than six activities

5. More than ten activities

Indicator 4.3 Develops and utilizes communications channels with parents for the purpose of setting forth school objectives

---

Comment:

The main focus of Indicator 4.3 is the existence of communications channels that are specifically devoted to setting forth school objectives to parents. Examples of communications channels might include but are not necessarily be limited to grade level curriculum nights, newsletter columns devoted specifically to school objectives, parent conferences, written statements of school mission, written statements of instructional objectives for each grade level in each basic skill area, and school activities devoted to skill mastery that require parent participation and/or homework policy.

SCALE OF DESCRIPTORS:

1. No communications channels exist for the purpose of setting forth school objectives.

2. At least three communications channels exist for the purpose of setting forth school objectives.

3. At least six communications channels exist for the purpose of setting forth school objectives.

4. At least ten communications channels exist for the purpose of setting forth school objectives.

5. In addition to the ten communications channels that exist for the purpose of setting forth school objectives, the principal and faculty evaluate, refine, and develop additional means of communicating with parents regarding school objectives.

KEY POINTS IN DESCRIPTORS:

1. No channels

2. At least three channels

3. At least six channels

4. At least ten channels

5. At least ten channels and an evaluation, refining, and development process

STEP FIVE: Set high expectations for the staff.

Indicator 5.1 Assists teachers in setting and reaching personal and professional goals related to the improvement of school instruction and monitors the successful completion of these goals

Comment:

The main focus of Indicator 5.1 is the active participation of the principal in the goal-setting process with teachers. Assistance is provided by the principal to the teachers in reaching stated goals, and the information obtained in the goal-setting process is utilized in teacher evaluation.

SCALE OF DESCRIPTORS:

1. Principal does not require that teachers set personal and professional goals.

2. Principal requires that teachers set personal and professional goals but is not involved in the goal-setting process and does not require that goals be related to the improvement of instruction.

3. Principal requires that teachers set personal and professional goals and that goals be related to the improvement of instruction but does not assist in the attainment of goals or monitor completion.

4. Principal requires that teachers set personal and professional goals in a cooperative way, insists that these goals be related to the improvement of instruction, and provides assistance in the attainment of these goals.

5. Principal requires that all teachers develop personal and professional goals related to the improvement of instruction in cooperation with the principal. Principal provides assistance to the teacher in the attainment of goals, monitors the completion of the goals, and utilizes the information in the evaluation process.

KEY POINTS IN DESCRIPTORS:

1. No goal setting by teachers

2. Goal setting not necessarily related to the improvement of instruction; no principal input, assistance, monitoring, or evaluation

3. Goal setting related to improvement of instruction; principal input; no principal assistance, monitoring, or evaluation

4. Goal setting related to improvement of instruction; principal input and assistance; no principal monitoring or evaluation

5. Goal setting related to improvement of instruction; principal input, assistance, monitoring, and evaluation

---

Indicator 5.2 Makes regular classroom observations in all classrooms, both informal (drop-in visits of varying length with no written or verbal feedback to teacher) and formal (visits where observation data is recorded and communicated to teacher)

Comment:

The main focus of Indicator 5.2 is on the quantity of classroom observations (both formal and informal).

SCALE OF DESCRIPTORS:

1. Principal makes formal classroom observations once every two years or less and never visits the classroom informally.

2. Principal makes at least one formal classroom observation per year and occasionally drops in informally.

3. Principal makes two formal classroom observations per year and at least one monthly informal observation.

4. Principal makes three formal classroom observations per year and at least two monthly informal observations.

5. Principal makes four or more classroom observations per year and visits the classroom informally at least once each week.

KEY POINTS IN DESCRIPTORS:

1. Minimal formal observations and no informal observations

2. One yearly formal observation and minimal informal observations

3. Two yearly formal observations and two monthly informal observations

4. Three yearly formal observations and two monthly informal observations

5. Four yearly formal observations and weekly informal observations

Indicator 5.3 Engages in preplanning of classroom observations

Comment:

The main focus of Indicator 5.3 is the quality of preplanning prior to a formal classroom observation where information is being collected relative to improvement of instruction.

SCALE OF DESCRIPTORS:

1. There is no typical pattern. Principal stops in to visit in no systematic fashion. Teachers are not usually aware that the principal will visit.

2. Principal generally informs teachers before an observation. A lesson may be observed, but there is no specific request for such on the part of the principal.

3. Principal and teacher arrange together for a specific observation time. A complete lesson is usually observed.

4. Principal and teacher arrange together for a specific observation time. A discussion is held regarding the lesson plan for the observation, but no attempts are ever made by the principal to focus on specific curricular areas or instructional strategies (e.g., cooperative grouping in a reading lesson or questioning techniques used on target students). A complete lesson is always observed.

5. Principal and teacher plan the focus of each observation at a preconference. Principal frequently takes the initiative regarding the focus of the observation and relates it to building goals and objectives. A specific observation time is scheduled. A complete lesson is always observed.

KEY POINTS IN DESCRIPTORS:

1. No teacher awareness of observation; no preplanning conference; random observation of incomplete lessons

2. Teacher awareness of observation; no preplanning conference; observation includes both complete and incomplete lessons

3. Teacher awareness of observation; no preplanning conference; observation always includes complete lesson

4. Teacher awareness of observation; preplanning conference without specific focus by principal; complete lesson always observed

5. Teacher awareness of observation; preplanning conference with frequent principal initiative regarding subject of observation; complete lesson always observed

Indicator 5.4 Engages in postobservation conferences that focus on the improvement of instruction (District requirements for frequency and procedures with regard to teacher evaluation may vary and substantially impact the interpretation of this indicator. The scale of descriptors describes a best-case scenario.)

Comment:

The main focus of Indicator 5.4 is the quantity and quality of postobservation conferences that focus on the improvement of instruction.

SCALE OF DESCRIPTORS:

1. Principal engages in a postobservation conference once every two years or less with each teacher, with little or no focus on the improvement of instruction

2. Principal engages in one postobservation conference with each teacher every year but rarely focuses on the improvement of instruction

3. Principal engages in two postobservation conferences with each teacher every year and provides one-way information about the improvement of instruction

4. Principal engages in three postobservation conferences with each teacher every year, engaging in both one-way and two-way communication about the improvement of instruction

5. Principal engages in four postobservation conferences with each teacher every year, engaging in both one-way and two-way communication about the improvement of instruction. Joint plans for follow-up in the classroom are developed with principal providing instructional resources and assistance

1. One conference every two years with no focus on improvement of instruction

2. One conference every year with rare focus on improvement of instruction

3. Two conferences every year with one-way communication about improvement of instruction

4. Three conferences every year with both one-way and two-way communication about the improvement of instruction

5. Four conferences every year with both one-way and two-way communication about the improvement of instruction; joint plans for follow-up with instructional resources and assistance provided

Indicator 5.5 Provides thorough, defensible, and insightful evaluations, making recommendations for personal and professional growth goals according to individual needs

Comment:

The main focus of Indicator 5.5 is the quality of the evaluation provided by the principal.

SCALE OF DESCRIPTORS:

1. All teachers receive nearly identical written evaluation ratings from the principal. There is no indication that evaluation is based on direct observation or supporting evidence, and no suggestions for improvement or growth are made.

2. Most teachers receive nearly identical written evaluation ratings from the principal. There is little indication that evaluation is based on direct observation or supporting evidence, and no suggestions for improvement or growth are made.

3. Although gradations of written evaluation ratings exist, these gradations appear to have no relationship to teacher performance or supporting evidence. No suggestions for improvement or growth are made.

4. Most teachers receive thorough written evaluations based on direct observation and supporting evidence. Principal makes few suggestions for improvement and growth.

5. Each teacher receives a thoughtful written evaluation based on direct observation and supporting evidence. Principal includes suggestions for improvement and growth tailored to individual needs.

KEY POINTS IN DESCRIPTORS:

1. Uniform evaluations for all teachers, no supporting evidence, no suggestions for growth

2. Nearly uniform evaluations for all teachers, no supporting evidence, no suggestions for growth

3. Gradation of evaluation ratings, no supporting evidence, no suggestions for growth

4. Thorough evaluations for all teachers, supporting evidence, no suggestions for growth

5. Thorough evaluations for all teachers, supporting evidence, suggestions for growth

Indicator 5.6 Engages in direct teaching in the classrooms of his/her school

Comment:

The main focus of Indicator 5.6 is the number of times the principal teaches a lesson observed by the classroom teacher in his/her school. This indicator does not include reading stories aloud or assisting teachers. It focuses on lesson preparation and the opportunity for the classroom teacher to engage in an observation of this lesson.

SCALE OF DESCRIPTORS:

1. Principal engages in no direct teaching in the classroom.

2. Principal engages in direct teaching in any classroom at least once per year.

3. Principal engages in direct teaching in any classroom at least two to four times per year.

4. Principal engages in direct teaching in any classroom at least five to ten times per year.

5. Principal engages in direct teaching in the classroom more than ten times per year.

KEY POINTS IN DESCRIPTORS:

1. No direct teaching

2. One episode of direct teaching

3. Two to four episodes of direct teaching

4. Five to ten episodes of direct teaching

5. More than ten episodes of direct teaching

STEP SIX: Develop teacher leaders.

Indicator 6.1 Schedules, plans, or facilitates regular meetings of all types (planning, problem solving, decision making, or in-service/training) among teachers to address instructional issues

Comment:

The main focus of Indicator 6.1 is both the quantity and quality of meetings that discuss instructional issues.

SCALE OF DESCRIPTORS:

1. Few meetings are held, instructional issues are never discussed, and no shared decision making or collaboration occurs.

2. Meetings are held on an "as needed" basis, instructional issues are rarely discussed, and no shared decision making or collaboration occurs.

3. Meetings are regularly scheduled, instructional issues are sometimes discussed, and some shared decision making and collaboration occur.

4. Meetings are regularly scheduled, instructional issues are discussed on an "as needed" basis, and some shared decision making and collaboration are evident.

5. Meetings of all types are regularly scheduled, instructional issues are discussed on a continuing basis, and shared decision making and collaboration characterize all meetings.

KEY POINTS IN DESCRIPTORS

1. Few meetings held, no instructional discussions, no shared decision making or collaboration

2. Few meetings held, rare instructional discussions, no shared decision making or collaboration

3. Regularly scheduled meetings, some instructional discussions, some shared decision making and collaboration

4. Regularly scheduled meetings, regularly scheduled instructional discussions, some shared decision making and collaboration

5. Regularly scheduled meetings with continuing discussion of instructional issues, collaboration and shared decision making

Indicator 6.2 Provides opportunities for and training in collaboration, shared decision making, coaching, mentoring, curriculum development, and making presentations

Comment:

The main focus of Indicator 6.2 is the provision of opportunities as well as provision of training in all areas of teacher leadership.

SCALE OF DESCRIPTORS:

1. Principal never provides opportunities or training for teachers to develop leadership skills.

2. Principal provides some opportunities and training for teachers to develop leadership skills but does so in a highly controlled and regulated fashion.

3. Principal provides some opportunities and training for teachers to develop leadership skills but permits a great deal of latitude in the exercise of these skills and does not utilize them or focus them in an organized way.

4. Principal provides a multitude of opportunities and training for teachers to develop leadership skills and utilizes these skills to improve instruction, coordinate with building mission, and improve student learning.

5. Principal provides a multitude of opportunities and training for teachers to develop leadership skills, utilizes them to continually improve instruction in classrooms, and has a school leadership team that participates in the continual improvement of the school.

KEY POINTS IN DESCRIPTORS:

1. No opportunities or training

2. Some opportunities and training but not relevant to needs

3. Opportunities and training provided that are relevant to faculty needs

4. Opportunities and training provided that are relevant to faculty needs and relates to improvement of instruction

5. Opportunities and training provided that are relevant to faculty needs; relate to improvement of instruction; are jointly planned, evaluated, and followed up; and include a systematic school improvement process under the leadership of a school team

Indicator 6.3 Provides motivation and resources for faculty members to engage in professional growth activities

Comment:

The focus of Indicator 6.3 is the encouragement provided by the principal to faculty members either by personal example or positive reinforcement, as well as the allocation of available resources to support professional growth activities.

SCALE OF DESCRIPTORS:

1. Principal never engages in personal professional growth activities and discourages teachers from doing so by failing to allocate resources for this activity in the budget.

2. Principal never engages in personal professional growth activities and, although monies are available for teacher activities, does not motivate or positively reinforce those teachers who take advantage of them.

3. Principal engages in personal professional growth activities and allocates resources for teachers to do so as well but does not motivate or positively reinforce those teachers who do so.

4. Principal engages in personal professional growth activities, allocates resources for teachers to do so as well, and motivates and positively reinforces those teachers who do so.

5. Principal engages in personal professional growth activities, allocates available resources for teachers to do so as well, motivates teachers to engage in activities that will benefit the building's instructional program, and utilizes their expertise in sharing with other teachers.

KEY POINTS IN DESCRIPTORS:

1. No personal growth activities, no motivation or reinforcement, no resources for teachers

2. No personal growth activities, no motivation or reinforcement, some allocation of resources

3. Personal growth activities, allocation of resources, no motivation or reinforcement

4. Personal growth activities, allocation of available resources, motivation and reinforcement

5. Personal growth activities, allocation of resources, motivation and reinforcement, utilization of teachers in building activities

STEP SEVEN: Maintain positive attitudes toward students, staff, and parents.

Indicator 7.1 Serves as an advocate of students and communicates with them regarding aspects of their school life

Comment:

The main focus of Indicator 7.1 is on the behaviors that the principal exhibits that give evidence of student advocacy and interaction with students. Behaviors might include lunch with individual students or groups; frequent appearances on the playground, in the lunchroom and hallways; sponsorship of clubs; availability to students who wish to discuss instructional or disciplinary concerns; knowledge of students' names and family relationships; addressing the majority of students by name; and willingness to listen to the student's side in a faculty/student problem. The preceding list is meant ONLY to suggest the types of behaviors that might be appropriate for consideration in this category.

SCALE OF DESCRIPTORS:

1. Principal does not feel that acting as a student advocate is an appropriate role of the principal and never interacts with students.

2. Principal does not feel that acting as a student advocate is an appropriate role of the principal and rarely interacts with students.

3. Principal does not feel that acting as a student advocate is an appropriate role of the principal but engages in at least three behaviors that encourage communication between student and principal.

4. Principal feels that acting as a student advocate is an appropriate role of the principal and engages in at least six behaviors that encourage communication between student and principal.

5. Principal feels that acting as a student advocate is an appropriate role of the principal, engages in at least six behaviors that encourage communication between student and principal, and has established some means of receiving input from students regarding their opinions of school life.

KEY POINTS IN DESCRIPTORS:

1. No role as an advocate, no interaction with students

2. No role as an advocate, rare interaction with students

3. No role as an advocate, three behaviors that encourage communication

4. Role as an advocate, six behaviors that encourage communication

5. Role as an advocate, six behaviors that encourage communication, some means of receiving student input

Indicator 7.2 Encourages open communication among staff members and maintains respect for differences of opinion

Comment:

The main focus of Indicator 7.2 is on the behaviors that the principal exhibits that give evidence of maintenance of open communication among staff members and respect for differences of opinion. Behaviors might include an open-door policy in the principal's office, acceptance of unpopular ideas and negative feedback from faculty, provision of channels for faculty members to voice grievances or discuss problems, and/or provision of channels for faculty members to discuss their work with each other. The preceding list is meant ONLY to suggest the types of behaviors that might be appropriate for consideration in this category.

SCALE OF DESCRIPTORS:

1. Principal does not encourage open communication among staff members and considers differences of opinion to be a sign of disharmony within the organization.

2. Principal supports open communication but is rarely available for informal encounters with staff members. Appointments must be scheduled, meeting agendas are tightly maintained, and the flow of information and opinions is artificially controlled.

3. Principal supports open communication and is available for informal encounters with staff members. Principal is not responsive, however, to problems, questions, or disagreements, and shuts off communication of this nature.

4. Principal supports open communication and is available for informal encounters with staff members. Principal is responsive to problems, questions, or disagreements and encourages staff members to work through differences of opinion in positive ways.

5. Principal supports open communication and is available for informal encounters with staff members. An "open-door" policy exists with regard to all problems, questions, and disagreements. Principal structures a variety of opportunities for faculty members to interact both formally and informally, encouraging interaction between grade levels/departments/instructional teams.

1. Discourages open communication

2. Exhibits few behaviors that encourage open communication

3. Exhibits some behaviors that encourage open communication

4. Exhibits many behaviors that encourage open communication and facilitates problem solving among staff members

5. Exhibits many behaviors that encourage open communication, facilitates problem solving among staff members, and structures many opportunities for staff interaction

Indicator 7.3 Demonstrates concern and openness in the consideration of student, teacher, and/or parent problems and participates in the resolution of such problems where appropriate

Comment:

The main focus of Indicator 7.3 is the behaviors the principal exhibits in the consideration of problems.

SCALE OF DESCRIPTORS:

1. Principal does not wish to be involved in the consideration of student, teacher, and/or parent problems.

2. Principal is willing to be involved in the consideration of student, teacher, and/or parent problems but is largely ineffective because of poor communication and human relations skills.

3. Principal is willing to be involved in the consideration of student, teacher, and/or parent problems and is sometimes effective in bringing problems to resolution. Exhibits average communication and human relations skills.

4. Principal is willing to be involved in the consideration of student, teacher, and/or parent problems and is usually effective in bringing problems to resolution. Exhibits excellent communication and human relations skills.

5. Principal is willing to be involved in the consideration of student, teacher, and/or parent problems and is nearly always effective in bringing problems to resolution. Exhibits outstanding communication and human relations skills. Has established procedures jointly with faculty for the resolution of problems.

KEY POINTS IN DESCRIPTORS:

1. No involvement

2. Some involvement, ineffective problem solver

3. Involvement, average problem-solving skills

4. Involvement, excellent problem-solving skills

5. Involvement, outstanding problem-solving skills

Indicator 7.4 Models appropriate human relations skills

Comment:

The main focus of Indicator 7.4 is the variety of appropriate human relations skills that are exhibited by the principal. Behaviors MUST include but are not necessarily limited to establishing a climate of trust and security for students and staff; respecting the rights of students, parents, and staff; handling individual relationships tactfully and with understanding; and accepting the dignity and worth of individuals without regard to appearance, race, creed, sex, ability or disability, or social status.

SCALE OF DESCRIPTORS:

1. Principal has almost no human relations skills.

2. Principal has marginal human relations skills.

3. Principal has average human relations skills.

4. Principal has excellent human relations skills.

5. Principal has outstanding human relations skills.

KEY POINTS IN DESCRIPTORS:

1. Principal exhibits none of the behaviors listed in the Comment section.

2. Principal exhibits only one or two of the behaviors listed in the Comment section and often has difficulty with tasks that involve human interaction.

3. Principal exhibits two or three of the behaviors listed in the Comment section and is usually successful with tasks that involve human interaction.

4. Principal exhibits three or four of the behaviors listed in the Comment section and is frequently successful with tasks that involve human interaction.

5. Principal exhibits all of the behaviors listed in the Comment section as well as many other behaviors associated with good human relations and is almost always successful with tasks that involve human interaction.

Indicator 7.5 Develops and maintains high morale

Comment:

The main focus of Indicator 7.5 is the variety of behaviors exhibited by the principal that contribute to the development and maintenance of high morale. Behaviors might include but not necessarily be limited to involvement of staff in planning, encouragement of planned social events, openness in the dissemination of information, equity in the division of responsibility and allocation of resources, opportunities for achievement, recognition for achievements, involvement of the staff in problem solving, and assistance and support with personal and professional problems.

SCALE OF DESCRIPTORS:

1. Morale is nonexistent in the school building. Principal exhibits none of the behaviors listed in the Comment section. There is little unity among staff members, leading to competition, clique formation, destructive criticism, disagreement, and verbal quarreling.

2. Morale is marginal in the school building. Principal exhibits few of the behaviors listed in the Comment section. Although fewer visible signs of disunity are evident, faculty members nevertheless do not work well together and have negative feelings about their work.

3. Morale is average. Although there are no visible signs of disunity as seen in Descriptor One, teachers work largely as individuals, rarely working together cooperatively with enthusiasm and positive feelings.

4. Morale is excellent. Morale-building behaviors by the principal result in teachers working together to share ideas and resources, to identify instructional problems, to define mutual goals, and to coordinate their activities.

5. Morale is outstanding. Morale-building behaviors by the principal result in teachers working together in a highly effective way while gaining personal satisfaction from their work. Principal has identified specific activities that build morale and systematically engages in these activities.

KEY POINTS IN DESCRIPTORS:

1. Nonexistent morale

2. Marginal morale

3. Average morale

4. Excellent morale

5. Outstanding morale

Indicator 7.6 Systematically collects and responds to student, staff, and parent concerns

Comment:

The main focus of Indicator 7.6 is the responsiveness of the principal to the regularly solicited and collected concerns of students, staff, and parents. Examples of vehicles used to collect information might include but are not necessarily limited to one-on-one conferences, parent or faculty advisory committees, student council meetings, suggestion boxes, and quality circles.

SCALE OF DESCRIPTORS:

1. No information is collected from students, staff, or parents. Principal is unresponsive to concerns of these groups.

2. Although information is sporadically collected from groups, principal is largely ineffective in responding to concerns.

3. Information is systematically collected from at least one of the three groups, and the principal is effective in responding to concerns.

4. Information is systematically collected from at least two of the three groups, and the principal is effective in responding to concerns.

5. Information is systematically collected from students, staff, and parents; principal is effective in responding to concerns; and information is utilized in planning and implementing change.

KEY POINTS IN DESCRIPTORS:

1. No information, unresponsive principal

2. Sporadic information, ineffective principal

3. Systematic information from one group, effective principal

4. Systematic information from two groups, effective principal

5. Systematic information from three groups, effective principal, utilization of information to plan change

Indicator 7.7 Acknowledges appropriately the earned achievements of others

Comment:

The main focus in Indicator 7.7 is the variety of activities engaged in by the principal that demonstrate the ability to recognize the contributions of students, staff, and parents. Activities might include but are not necessarily limited to staff recognition programs, student award assemblies, certificates, congratulatory notes, phone calls, recognition luncheons, and newspaper articles.

SCALE OF DESCRIPTORS:

1. Principal engages in no recognition activities.

2. Principal engages in at least one recognition activity for one of the three groups.

3. Principal engages in at least one recognition activity for two of the three groups.

4. Principal engages in at least one recognition activity for all three groups.

5. In addition to a variety of recognition activities, the principal involves all three groups in recognition activities for one another.

KEY POINTS IN DESCRIPTORS:

1. No recognition activities

2. One recognition for one of three groups

3. One recognition for two of three groups

4. One recognition for each of the three groups

5. Many recognition activities, with focus on groups recognizing each other

RESPONSE FORM:
THE INSTRUCTIONAL LEADERSHIP BEHAVIORAL CHECKLIST

	NEVER	SELDOM	SOMETIMES	USUALLY	ALWAYS
Indicator 1.1:	1	2	3	4	5

Involves teachers in developing and implementing school instructional goals and objectives

	NEVER	SELDOM	SOMETIMES	USUALLY	ALWAYS
Indicator 1.2:	1	2	3	4	5

Incorporates the designated state and/or system curriculum in the development of instructional programs

Indicator 1.3:	1	2	3	4	5

Ensures that school and classroom activities are consistent with school instructional goals and objectives

Indicator 1.4:	1	2	3	4	5

Evaluates progress toward instructional goals and objectives

Indicator 2.1:	1	2	3	4	5

Works with teachers to improve the instructional program in their classrooms consistent with student needs

Indicator 2.2:	1	2	3	4	5

Bases instructional program development on sound research and practice

Indicator 2.3:	1	2	3	4	5

Applies appropriate formative procedures for evaluating the instructional program

Indicator 3.1:	1	2	3	4	5

Establishes high expectations for student achievement that are directly communicated to students, teachers, and parents

Indicator 3.2:	1	2	3	4	5

Establishes clear rules and expectations for the use of time allocated to instruction and monitors the effective use of classroom time

Indicator 3.3:	1	2	3	4	5

Establishes, implements, and evaluates with teachers and students (as appropriate) procedures and codes for handling and correcting discipline problems

Indicator 4.1:	1	2	3	4	5

Provides for systematic two-way communication with staff regarding the ongoing objectives and goals of the school

Indicator 4.2:	1	2	3	4	5

Establishes, supports, and implements activities that communicate to students the value and meaning of learning

Indicator 4.3:	1	2	3	4	5

Develops and utilizes communication channels with parents for the purpose of setting forth school objectives

Indicator 5.1:	1	2	3	4	5

Assists teachers in setting personal and professional goals related to the improvement of school instruction and monitors the successful completion of these goals

RESPONSE FORM:
THE INSTRUCTIONAL LEADERSHIP BEHAVIORAL CHECKLIST 2

	NEVER	SELDOM	SOMETIMES	USUALLY	ALWAYS
Indicator 5.2: Makes regular classroom observations in all classrooms, both informal and formal	1	2	3	4	5
Indicator 5.3: Engages in preplanning of classroom observations	1	2	3	4	5
Indicator 5.4: Engages in postobservation conferences that focus on the improvement of instruction	1	2	3	4	5
Indicator 5.5: Provides thorough, defensible, and insightful evaluations, making recommendations for personal and professional growth goals according to individual needs	1	2	3	4	5
Indicator 5.6: Engages in direct teaching in the classrooms of his or her school	1	2	3	4	5
Indicator 6.1: Schedules, plans, or facilitates regular meetings of all types (planning, problem solving, decision making, or inservice/training) between teachers to address instructional issues	1	2	3	4	5
Indicator 6.2: Provides opportunities for and training in collaboration, shared decision making, coaching, mentoring, curriculum development, and making presentations	1	2	3	4	5
Indicator 6.3: Provides motivation and resources for faculty members to engage in professional growth activities	1	2	3	4	5
Indicator 7.1: Serves as an advocate of students and communicates with them regarding aspects of their school life	1	2	3	4	5
Indicator 7.2: Encourages open communication among staff members and maintains respect for differences of opinion	1	2	3	4	5
Indicator 7.3: Demonstrates concern and openness in the consideration of student, teacher, and/or parent problems and participates in the resolution of such problems where appropriate	1	2	3	4	5
Indicator 7.4: Models appropriate human relations skills	1	2	3	4	5
Indicator 7.5: Develops and maintains high morale	1	2	3	4	5
Indicator 7.6: Systematically collects and responds to student, staff, and parent concerns	1	2	3	4	5
Indicator 7.7: Acknowledges appropriately the earned achievements of others	1	2	3	4	5

Index